ESCAPE
THE
RICH
TRAP

ESCAPE
THE
RICH
TRAP

THE PATH TO WEALTH THAT GETS YOU
OFF THE HAMSTER WHEEL

DAVID A. PEREZ

SAVIO
REPVBLIC

A SAVIO REPUBLIC BOOK
An Imprint of Post Hill Press
ISBN: 979-8-88845-791-7
ISBN (eBook): 979-8-88845-792-4

Escape the Rich Trap:
The Path to Wealth That Gets You Off the Hamster Wheel
© 2025 by David A. Perez
All Rights Reserved

Cover Design by Cody Corcoran

This book, as well as any other Savio Republic publications, may be purchased in bulk quantities at a special discounted rate. Contact orders@posthillpress.com for more information.

All people, locations, events, and situations are portrayed to the best of the author's memory. While all of the events described are true, many names and identifying details have been changed to protect the privacy of the people involved.

SAVIO
REPVBLIC

posthillpress.com
New York • Nashville
Published in the United States of America

1 2 3 4 5 6 7 8 9 10

TABLE OF CONTENTS

1

WHAT IS THE RICH TRAP?

I can already see the look on your face as you read the title of this book. "Escape the Rich Trap? Really?" You might be skeptical—and you should be. After all, we grow up believing that being rich is life's ultimate prize. That "rich" is the be-all and end-all of success. The big house, the luxury car, the lavish lifestyle—aren't those the things we're all supposed to strive for?

I know exactly how you feel because I've been there. Like you, I believed for most of my life that making a lot of money and living large was the whole point. I wanted to be rich, and I worked my ass off to achieve it. Eventually, I did make it. I had the money, the status, the lifestyle. And that's when I realized something unsettling: Being rich can actually be a trap—a "rich trap" that keeps you on a relentless hamster wheel, always running but never truly safe or free.

If that sounds strange, let me reassure you: Skepticism is good. I want you to question what I'm saying. In fact, questioning is the first step toward seeing that "rich" and "wealthy" are not the same thing. Being rich might mean you have flashy stuff, but it doesn't mean you have genuine security or freedom. Being wealthy, on the other hand, means building a foundation so solid that it can weather any financial storm. It means owning the Airbnb instead of just renting it. It means not just making money, but keeping it, growing it, and protecting it for the long haul.

Being Rich Versus Being Wealthy

Let's clear up the difference before we go any further. Rich people have plenty of cool things—cars, houses, fancy dinners at restaurants that require monthslong reservations, and trips to exotic resorts. Wealthy people may enjoy some of those same comforts, but what sets them apart is the invisible layer of security beneath it all. Wealthy people are stable because they've invested wisely and set themselves up with passive income and long-term financial plans. They know that their money works for them, not the other way around.

Rich people, on the other hand, are often cash-rich and investment-poor. They may be just one economic downturn, one big bill, or one unexpected twist of fate away from financial ruin. As I'll share with you, I discovered this truth firsthand—when I had it all and almost lost it all.

My Story: From Rags to Riches to Wealthy

I grew up in a small town on the southernmost edge of Texas, minutes from the Mexican border. I was born to a seventeen-year-old mother, never met my father, and was raised by my grandparents. I'm Mexican by ethnicity, yet I was born with albinism—my skin is white as snow, and I have low vision, which meant growing up I was often treated as "different." I spent my childhood partly sheltered, partly bullied, and always feeling out of place. But I didn't have a bad childhood. My parents (grandparents, officially) did their best and filled my life with love and support, even though we never had much money.

As I grew older, I rebelled against the idea of being seen as different, of being coddled and told what I could or couldn't do. Money, I believed, would solve all my problems. If I was rich, I'd never be dependent on anyone. Rich would equal freedom.

I wasn't sure how to get there, though. My early attempts at college were failures, and I drifted until I stumbled into real estate in the mid-2000s. I saw people making fast fortunes—people who suddenly appeared superrich. But when the market crashed, those fortunes disappeared overnight. I learned a valuable lesson: If all your wealth can vanish that easily, maybe you were never truly wealthy in the first place.

Eventually, I pivoted into the tax business. Starting in 2008, I opened one office and did well—so well that I thought I'd mastered it instantly. I quickly expanded, opening multiple offices until I had fifteen. On the outside, I looked like a major success story: big operations, big money, a big life. But beneath the surface, I was financing that expansion with borrowed money. I was spending and living large. I was "rich," but not really wealthy. When a gigantic $142,000 tax bill showed up, I didn't have the resources to cover it. I almost filed for bankruptcy.

That crisis forced me to confront the truth. I needed to really learn about money, taxes, and how the wealthy protect and grow their fortunes. Over time, I studied, learned, and transformed my approach, not just to build wealth for myself, but also to help others do the same. Today, I work with clients who owe tens or even hundreds of thousands of dollars in taxes, helping them rethink their finances, escape the rich trap, and become wealthy.

Building Generational Wealth: The Path Forward

Here's the critical distinction we've been working toward: Rich is fragile. Wealth is secure. The wealthy are not just about having money; they're about using money wisely. They create passive income, diversify their investments, leverage tax strategies, and think generationally. While the rich have a flashy car in the driveway, the wealthy own the lot next door and build rental properties on it.

I've helped thousands of people learn this lesson. Often, they feel a sense of shock when they realize they've been doing it "wrong" all these years, always chasing bigger paychecks or fancier toys without building a stable foundation. But there are answers. This book provides the exact steps you need to start building wealth right now, wherever you are.

My approach simplifies the process. I'll help you:

1. Recognize the rich trap and the dangers it poses for you and your family.
2. Implement a step-by-step process to get unstuck.
3. Initiate a personalized tax plan so you can keep more of what you earn.
4. Develop an investment strategy tailored to your income that increases your cash flow.

5. Use my "wealthy formula" to allocate your income to five core buckets of wealth that will secure your future for generations.

These five steps will guide you toward a lifetime of wealth for you and your family. But understanding the difference between rich and wealthy is just the beginning. In the coming chapters, we'll delve deeper into how to change your mindset, where and how to invest, how to leverage smart tax strategies, and how to protect and pass on your wealth to ensure it lasts beyond your own lifetime.

Now that you understand what the rich trap is—and the critical importance of focusing on wealth rather than fleeting riches—let's move forward. In the next chapter, we'll explore how wealthy thinking differs from rich thinking and get you started on the mental shift that underpins everything else to come.

Step-by-step, we'll put this all into action. Your journey out of the rich trap and into a life of genuine, lasting wealth starts here.

Chapter 1: What Is the Rich Trap?

Wealth Reflections

1. What early beliefs about "richness" might be holding you back from understanding true wealth?

2. How have you focused on appearances or short-term gains rather than building long-term security?

3. In what ways could redefining "success" as long-term stability rather than immediate rewards change your financial decisions?

2

BEING WEALTHY STARTS BY THINKING WEALTHY

Wealth is built over time. This is why being rich becomes the trap. You can see the impact of making money the moment it hits your account, and that instant gratification makes it easy to fall into the trap we discussed in chapter 1.

Here's a good example:

There's a famous psychology experiment called the marshmallow test. The test is a simple one. Preschool children around four years of age were told they could have a treat, a marshmallow. They could eat one marshmallow right away, or, if they waited fifteen minutes, they could have two. The purpose of the study was to determine not only how well preschool children could "delay gratification"—in other words, display self-control—but also how that ability translated across their lifespan.

The results were pretty amazing. The children who were able to delay gratification—that is, the children who waited fifteen minutes to double the number of treats—ended up doing better in a wide range of things later in life, from earning more money to being in healthier, more stable relationships.

I'm telling you about this study, not because I want you to eat fewer sugary snacks. I'm telling you about it because it illustrates a key difference between being rich and being wealthy, which we began exploring in the previous chapter. The rich people are more apt to be the ones who eat that first marshmallow right away. The rich people can't control themselves. They see something that looks good, and they snap it up without thinking about the future consequences. The wealthy people, on the other hand, are the ones who are always thinking about the future consequences. They're not focused on what's right in front of them; they're thinking three moves ahead.

The researchers of the marshmallow test determined that the children who delayed gratification had better life outcomes because they had more planful, goal-oriented thinking. You know what that means? Those kids were thinking wealthy. The kids who immediately plowed back the first marshmallow they saw were thinking rich. Just consider for a second the difference in assets these two sets of kids would accrue over the course of a day.

Let's say we ran this experiment every fifteen minutes for an hour. The kids without self-control—the rich kids—would eat the first marshmallow presented to them each time. That means they would get four marshmallows total. The kids who displayed self-control—the wealthy kids—would find a way to delay their gratification for fifteen minutes each time and would get two marshmallows. They would end up with eight marshmallows at the end of the hour. Now, let's say we ran this every hour over the course of a day. Four marshmallows multiplied by twenty-four hours for the rich kids equals ninety-six marshmallows by day's end. The wealthy kids are accruing eight marshmallows an hour, so multiplied by twenty-four totals one hundred ninety-two marshmallows for the day.

If we project this one-day experiment over the course of a full year, we will see that the rich kids end up with 35,040 marshmallows. The wealthy kids, on the other hand, end up with 70,080. So, what at first didn't seem like a big difference—the rich kids get one marshmallow, the wealthy kids, two, for a difference of one measly marshmallow—ends up over the course of a year to be that wealthy kids hauled in an additional 35,040 marshmallows than the rich kids. That's a lot of marshmallows!

The thing is, in the real world, although the stakes are a lot higher than marshmallows, the premise is exactly the same. People who can set goals and think ahead do far better in life than those who don't. That's why the very first step in building generational wealth is to start thinking wealthy rather than thinking rich. Thinking rich not only will leave you with less but also will leave you more exposed. It will, as we discussed in chapter 1, leave you trapped! Let me tell you about this guy I knew in real estate who got sucked into the trap.

This guy started his career as a marriage counselor and actually had a successful business. But he was a spender, not a saver, not a planner. It didn't matter for a while because his business was doing well. He was making money. It was during the early 2000s, and real estate was going through the roof—everyone was making money. So he decided he wanted a piece of the action.

He bought a property that immediately jumped in value, so he bought another, and then another. Housing prices at this time just kept going higher and higher, so if you weren't thinking it through, thinking ahead, it was easy to get caught up in the mania, which is exactly what he did. His wife wanted a dream home, so he built it for her. He wanted a Ferrari, so he bought one. He was scooping up vacation rental homes in Florida like they were ice cream. As he told me, "I was living such a great life! I had it all—the home, the cars, the vacations, going out all the time. I was on top of the world."

Then the world changed, as it always does. The real estate market crashed. Then everything crashed. Because he was living rich (rather than wealthy), he was leveraging all these properties on variable-rate mortgages. Variable rates are called variable for a reason—it means they change over time. But if you're just gobbling up that first marshmallow you see, you're not thinking about how that 2.0 percent interest rate today might be 5.0 percent tomorrow. So not only did his property values tank, but also his interest rates all shot up. He was underwater on everything.

Suddenly, the bill came due on his fancy new home, the fancy car, and all these properties he'd purchased—but he couldn't pay it. He had no reserves, no savings. In short, he had no real wealth. He was just living rich. And he was trapped.

Long, sad story short, he lost everything. The banks came for everything he owned, put liens on his house, his properties, his car. He sank into a depression and battled lawsuits for years. He was still dealing with the fallout in 2023—fifteen years later. It's only recently that he's been able to start piecing his life back together again.

I'm not telling you this story to depress you. I'm telling you this as a cautionary tale. The rich trap isn't something I made up. It's real. And if you get caught in it, it can ruin your life. The rich trap is so dangerous because everything might look and feel great on the surface. He thought he had it all. But he didn't realize how close he was to going broke until it happened. That's the same for most people. On the outside, everything looks solid. On the inside, you're teetering on the edge of disaster.

But you don't want everything to just look solid. You want it to be solid. And for it to be solid, you need to be wealthy, not rich. And to be wealthy, you need to think wealthy. The question, then, is: How do you do that? Let's start by seeing how close you are to the edge yourself.

Are You in the Rich Trap?

We all have blind spots, including me, which I've already told you about! The tricky thing with blind spots is, well, they're blind spots—meaning, you can't see them. If you knew about them already, they wouldn't be blind spots; they'd be "seen spots." So what we want to do here is check your blind spots. See what you're aware of and maybe what you're not aware of. To do this, I'm going to ask you a few questions. Ready?

If another economic shift came today, if another recession happened like the Great Recession of 2008 or another pandemic hit and everything in the world just shut down and there was no government assistance and there was no handout, how far could you go? How far would your money take you?

This isn't a question for only business owners either. Obviously, if you're a business owner or an entrepreneur, yes, you want to understand how a huge shift in the economy would impact you. And I don't mean how it would impact your business. I mean, how a shift in the economy would impact you—personally. How would it impact your personal economy? Could you survive even if your business didn't?

But the same question goes for nonbusiness owners, for employees. If you're an employee and you work for a major corporation, how would the company be impacted and how would that impact you? Is the industry recession-proof? How bulletproof have you made yourself? Have you skilled up? Have you made something out of yourself so people need you? Have you been using the money you're earning to make investments? Are you thinking long term or week to week, month to month?

Chances are, if you think in terms of weeks or months for any of these questions, you're in the rich trap. You have some nice things, some luxury items. You keep your wardrobe up-to-date. You get compliments on your shoes or your shirt or your dress when you go out. But if you lost your job or your business tanked, you would too. That's the rich trap!

Many people might make half a million dollars a year because the husband and the wife each make $250,000, and they live a great life, but they're one paycheck away from being broke. I can't even tell you how many clients I've had who are earning a very nice salary—$300, $400, $500 grand a year—but they have no assets, no investments, no savings.

Sure, they're rich, but that's not a place I want to be living. Those same people often have million-dollar homes. They have two luxury cars (because having only one isn't rich, right?). What happens if one of them loses their job? Suddenly, that mortgage that was easy to pay with $500,000 coming in every year is impossible to afford with only half that. Those car payments that nobody was thinking about last week suddenly are all they can think about.

And when things go south in our personal economy, we automatically think about the big things—the house, the car, and so forth. But a lot of the pain for people stuck in the rich trap comes in the day-to-day. The pain comes from the drastic change in lifestyle that rich people have become accustomed to. It's easy to go out to eat every night on $500,000 when you know your mortgage will be paid, and there's no problem forking over the cash for the utility bill to heat and cool your 4,000-square-foot home. But it's impossible to eat out every night and pay all those same bills when you're only earning $250,000. There's also the inability to go shopping for new clothes as much as you're used to or even to make the smaller purchases, like a latte on the way to work each day. When you're in the rich trap, everything in your life can change in the blink of an eye.

So, if it all stopped today—if you lost your business or your job, or your partner got sick and couldn't work anymore—where would you get money from? Rich people have no answer to this. If you can't answer this question, officially consider yourself in the rich trap. Don't worry, we'll get you out soon enough! Because soon you will have an answer, like a wealthy person. Wealthy people could answer this question, no problem.

In the first chapter, we briefly discussed the difference between rich and wealthy. I told you that rich people vacation at Airbnbs, and wealthy people own them. The slightly more technical answer is wealthy people have passive income that exceeds their lifestyle and liabilities; rich people do not. That's the real difference. When there's a downturn in the economy or when something goes terribly wrong in someone's personal life, a wealthy person has the passive income and assets to keep going as they always have. A rich person's life will be completely turned upside down. Their standard of living would go way down because, rather than building wealth, they've been living in the rich trap.

Let's not do that anymore. Let's free ourselves from the trap. Let's start thinking wealthy!

Rich People Spend, Wealthy People Invest

Okay, so a common theme we've explored so far is that rich people might look safe and financially secure, but wealthy people are safe and financially secure. If we go back to the start of this chapter and the kids taking the marshmallow test, we saw that the profound difference between the kids who ate the first marshmallow versus the kids who waited fifteen minutes to double the number of marshmallows they would get comes down to the ability to delay gratification. But it's easy to see these results and think that some kids (and some adults) naturally have more self-control than others. But is it that simple? What four-year-old isn't going to be tempted by a fluffy, sugary marshmallow? It's sugar! They're four years old! They want it!

No, it would be a mistake to just chalk it up to natural self-control. The most critical takeaway from this famous experiment is actually the factor that underlies the differences between the two groups of children—the ability to think ahead, that is, having a goal and coming up with a strategy to achieve that goal. During the marshmallow test experiment, researchers noted a number of different strategies kids used to make it through the fifteen minutes they had to wait to collect the second marshmallow treat. To avoid eating the first marshmallow right away, some kids closed their eyes, some put their head down, some distracted themselves by looking around the room or talking to themselves.

In short, these children understood that, as much as they wanted that first amazing marshmallow sitting in front of them, they would be much better off waiting fifteen minutes to double their prize and their pleasure. To get themselves from a nice-looking Point A to an even better looking and more prosperous Point B, they came up with strategies to pass the time and help them maintain their self-control. This is exactly what wealthy people do and exactly what rich people do not do. Ultimately, wealthy people make better decisions than rich people, and so from this point forward, you're going to make better decisions too. You're going to start thinking like a wealthy person.

A fundamental difference between the way rich people think and the way wealthy people think comes down to money. Rich people think about money as a way to get things. Wealthy people think about money as a way to get more money. Basically, rich people spend money, whereas wealthy people invest money. This means that rich people are busy losing money while wealthy people are busy making it. The faster you can make the leap from rich-people thinking to wealthy-people thinking, the faster you will be on your way to financial security and building generational wealth. Let me give you some examples of what I mean to illustrate the difference.

Rich people like to buy things. After all, we're programmed our whole lives to consume, right? From the time we start crawling, we're bombarded with flashy, cool things that we're supposed to want. It starts with toys, then as we get older, it becomes name-brand clothes, the latest skin care products, the coolest sneakers. The older we get, the bigger the things are we're supposed to want—the newest iPhone, the hottest car, an apartment in the trendiest neighborhood. And so, for people who end up making a lot of money, it makes sense they would want to get as much stuff as they can. This is especially true for people who don't come from money, who weren't born into money, who watched everyone around them get all this cool stuff while they went without. That's why you see the old cliché of "new money" versus "old money."

"New money" equals the rich. They have just recently experienced all this disposable income and can suddenly buy anything they want—and so they do. They buy and buy and buy. They are often first-generation rich people. "Old money" equals the wealthy. These people grew up with money, come from generational wealth. They don't need to buy everything they see because it's not new to them. They already have whatever they want and don't need to buy anything more to flex or show off. Old money is multigenerational. That's our goal—to build multigenerational wealth. And it's going to start with you!

But to do that, to take the first step, you have to resist the impulse to spend. Because, if you noticed, all the stuff I listed above that we're socialized from the cradle to want—the toys, the clothes, the phones, the cars—those things aren't investments. You lose money at the time of purchase because they depreciate as soon as you claim ownership. The instant you drive a new car off the lot, it depreciates in value. You've lost a couple thousand dollars before you even drive a mile down the road. That's an extreme example, but it's actually the same for pretty much any material item you buy. As soon as you walk out of the store with your $6,000 Gucci bag, you might get half that if you were to resell it on eBay. Clothes are essentially worthless once the tags come off. We can go straight down the line.

Then, of course, there are the daily trips to Starbucks for breakfast and Shake Shack for lunch and Ruth's Chris for dinner. Every time you eat out, you've spent money you will never get back again. Every time you drop one hundred dollars on the bar to buy you and your friends a round of drinks, that's money lost forever. To get it back, you have to earn it back. And if you don't have a wealth-generating strategy in place, that means you have to work to get that money back.

Ultimately, it's a losing proposition, this cycle of earning and spending money. Just like the kids who ate the first marshmallow, there's no delaying of gratification, no impulse control. Just constant spending and trying to earn back enough money to spend some more. It's all part of the rich trap because sooner or later something's going to shift, something's going to change, and that delicate balance is going to get thrown off. That's when bad things happen.

Instead of spending rich, we're going to shift your mindset to that of the wealthy who don't spend money—they invest it. Money, to the wealthy, is a tool to make more money. Later in this book, we're going to talk about bigger dedicated strategies to building wealth. But wealth creation starts with the daily. It starts in the way you think about money, generally. So we need to start thinking about money as an investment tool.

An easier way to think about this whole thing might be to use an old financial investment term—ROI, or return on investment. For every dollar you spend, what do you get in return? Ideally, every dollar you spend should pay a dividend of sorts. Every dollar should be a down payment on something that will generate wealth for you in the future. So, instead of spending a dollar and losing a dollar, you spend a dollar to gain $1.25 or $1.50 or $2.00 in the future.

How does this work in the real world, in your real life? You need to start thinking about what return you get on everything you spend money on. And I'm not saying you can't enjoy nice things or you can't enjoy a nice meal. Of course, you can. But rich people just spend mindlessly because, in the moment, they have the money to do so. Wealthy people, in contrast, consider the value of what they get in return for everything they do and everything they buy.

Let's take a seven-dollar coffee at Starbucks, for example. That's a lot of money to spend every day on some caffeine with processed, sugary syrup mixed in. It adds up over the course of a year. If you buy a seven-dollar coffee every day, you'll have spent $2,555 in a single year on that alone. Over the course of five years, that comes out to $12,775! And let's be honest, if you're going to Starbucks every day, you're probably buying a few other items, as well, over the course of a week—a four-dollar cake pop here, an eight-dollar egg sandwich there. It's far more likely that someone with a daily Starbucks habit is easily spending $15,000 over the course of five years. You have to ask yourself, "Is it worth it?"

That might be a difficult question to answer in isolation. You might be thinking, sure, it adds up, $15,000 over five years is a lot of money, but that Chocolate Caramel Frappuccino is so good! And that's fair. But what if you took that $15,000 and invested it in Apple or used it for a down payment on an investment property or a new business or private school for your kid? You might still say you'd go with the Frappuccino, and, again, that would be fair. But two things:

You're calculating your monetary investment in daily Starbucks coffee drinks against intangible returns; in this case, your pleasure or daily satisfaction with the product. It's a difficult comparison to make. You might be right that your pleasure in drinking your morning coffee is worth $15,000, but then that leads to the need to consider the second point.

Because it's so difficult to measure the ROI of your intangible pleasure gained from coffee drinks, to do a full accounting of this cost-benefit, you need to consider the intangible satisfaction you get from all your daily and weekly purchases. The weekly shopping sprees at Nordstrom, the fine dining, the nights out with friends. Once you tally it all up, is it all worth it? Is there any money that you might be better off spending elsewhere—perhaps on something that might earn you money in the future?

This is what I mean when I say you need to start thinking wealthy because this is exactly what wealthy people do. They assess the value and the ROI of everything they do. In fact, sometimes you can buy something and it's a complete waste of money—no ROI. But you can buy the exact same thing another time and get a huge return on your investment. Let me explain what I mean.

Let's stick with the Starbucks example. I don't drink coffee, so I, obviously, don't go to Starbucks ever, let alone every day. So, if I randomly bought a seven-dollar Frappuccino, it would clearly be money wasted. No ROI. However, if I was on my way to Starbucks to meet somebody who might possibly give me an idea that could change my business or my life or who might work for me or partner with me or connect me to a network or organization that might elevate my business, the seven dollars would be a great investment. I'd buy the coffee to play the game, and I'd buy the person I was meeting a coffee. The seven dollars could be seventy dollars, or even $170; it wouldn't matter, I wouldn't care, because it's dollars invested rather than dollars merely spent.

Let me give you another example of spending to invest.

I recently held a weekend company retreat. About fifty employees attended, all-expenses-paid. For the first day of the retreat, my company rented a convention center. We fed everyone a gourmet breakfast, lunch, and dinner and contracted some high-priced speakers to give presentations throughout the day. Then, for the next two days, I took participants to a beach, where all we did was hang out—eat, drink, get to know each other. Some of us went fishing in the morning on private boats. Some of the women went painting. We took out a boat and went out to dinner all together. My company went all out. I wanted the retreat to be informative and motivational, but I also wanted to create cohesion within the company. I wanted everyone to get to know each other on a personal level, a human level. I think that will make us a better company, a more profitable organization.

The final bill for the retreat was high. To be honest, higher than I was intending. But at the end of it all, to me, the $40,000 was worth it. Every dollar was an investment. I am investing in people and investing in opportunities for them to grow within our company, opportunities beyond what they would normally see.

And it paid off. In the weeks and months that followed, there was a different atmosphere in the office. People were motivated, talking to each other. It felt like they were a real team, with real energy; it wasn't some deadbeat office that no one wants to work at. Our team meetings have been more animated and livelier. People are reciting our company vision and core values every day. Our sales are way up. From the outside, spending on the retreat may look like lavish, rich spending, but it was actually an investment to attain greater wealth.

Of course, not every investment yields a return, but you invest because it opens up possibilities, it opens up opportunities for growth. That's wealthy thinking. People who spend mindlessly have zero opportunity for growth. That's rich thinking. For example, there are lots of companies out there doing very well, and there are a lot of newly rich owners who are going to throw wild, blowout parties with no clear purpose in mind. They're going to do it because they can. Period. That's not money invested, that's just money lost.

Whether you're running a business or running your personal economy, you always want to evaluate the ROI on whatever you spend. Is it a dollar spent, or is it a dollar invested? If you continue to ask yourself that question as you go about your daily life, you will steadily shift your mindset from thinking rich to thinking wealthy. It won't happen overnight, especially if you love the latest shiny new toys out there. And there will definitely be times when you just spend simply to spend and have fun and enjoy life, and, of course, that's okay too. But if you begin evaluating all your expenditures in terms of ROI, you will eventually just do so naturally, which is the first step in building generational wealth.

Go High or Go Low

To close out this chapter on thinking wealthy, I want to cover one last thing. Obviously, you have to spend money that will not result in any increased return on your investment. You need clothes. You need a car. You need things that will invariably depreciate rather than appreciate over time. That's life. And that's okay. But even here, you can think wealthy. You can look at ways to mitigate the loss, to minimize the depreciation of your purchase to your advantage.

To do this, always look at the very cheapest thing in a market or the most expensive. These two extremes—the lowest and the highest—will maximize your purchase and, at least to some extent, serve as an investment by mitigating your loss. I know you might be thinking, What the heck is he talking about? So let me give you a few examples.

Let's talk cars. When you're looking to buy a car, you know that it's a sunk investment. The moment you drive a car off the lot, it loses value, and it will continue to lose value the longer you drive it. I'm not telling you anything revolutionary here. I know you understand this already. But there is a way to minimize the depreciation or the overall value you gain from your car purchase. High-end cars, the luxury brands with the highest-end trim, will hold their value much better than cars with a lower sticker price. Why? Because there's always a market for the very best cars. People want the best, and there will always be people who have the money to spend on the best. If you get a luxury-brand vehicle, with the most expensive trim, the resale value of that car will remain far higher than that of less expensive, middle-of-the-road cars.

You might be saying, Well, once I buy the highest-end car that I love, I won't want to trade it in—ever. Great, don't! Buying the very best enables you to realize what we talked about earlier: intangible returns. You will have years of amazing driving experiences, traveling around in the very best of the best. You will have maximized your intangible returns with a luxury car, which isn't possible with a ho-hum, middle-of-the-road car. And, if you decide in a few years that you want to trade it in for a new car, the resale value of the luxury car will remain quite high because its value depreciates slowly since it's always in high demand. By buying the very best, you slowed your depreciation curve, which, ultimately, nets you more money that you can invest later. You can apply this logic to many of your purchases. The trade-in value on the highest-end products will always be higher because they are the most in demand—because they're the best.

The other way to maximize value is to go low, to spend as little as you can. Let's go back to the car example. By spending as little as you can on a new car, you, again, maximize your intangible return—that is, you know that you haven't spent a lot of money on a depreciating asset, so you're free not to care about the car at all. It's a carefree purchase. It will get you from Point A to Point B, and that's all you really care about. You can take pleasure in the carefreeness of it all. You also maximize your monetary value. A low-end car won't hold its value like a high-end car does, that's true, but you spent almost nothing on it to begin with, so you had far more money left in reserve to invest in things that will provide positive ROI, that will appreciate rather than depreciate, over time.

Anything in the middle of the market neither provides you with as much intangible return nor maximizes your monetary investment. The middle of any market has the least appeal. You can also apply this logic to running a business. Either strive to be the cheapest in the market or the most expensive. You do this for all the same reasons you go high or low with your purchases. People want the best, so they seek luxury and have the money to pay for it. People also want bargains, to get something for as little as possible, which is what the cheapest product on the market provides them.

On either end, you're giving people what they most want. Anything in the middle is a waste of time. For example, say you want to win in the pizza marketplace. Either be the cheapest pizza parlor or be the most expensive pizza parlor because everybody in the middle disappears. Nobody actively seeks out average.

By keeping these principles in mind, you're continuing the mindset shift we started in chapter 1. Now you understand that thinking wealthy, rather than rich, guides both your daily decisions and your long-term strategies. In the next chapter, we'll dive deeper into the process of building wealth, so you can start putting these ideas into action and secure a brighter future for yourself and your family.

Chapter 2: Being Wealthy Starts by Thinking Wealthy

Wealth Reflections

1. Where in your life have you chosen instant gratification over future security, and how can you shift that pattern?

2. How might thinking multiple steps ahead, rather than focusing only on the present, improve your financial outcomes?

3. What practical changes can you make to start thinking more like a wealthy person rather than a rich person?

3

THE PROCESS OF BUILDING WEALTH

In the first two chapters, we discussed what the rich trap is and then how to avoid this trap by learning how to think like a wealthy person, not a rich person. In this chapter, I want to drill down a bit further into this process. We've laid the foundational mindset you need for wealth creation (thinking like a wealthy person), and now we'll explore how that mindset translates into planning and action. In short, I want to teach you about the actual process of building wealth step-by-step.

Know What You're Investing In

Let's start by looking at one of the most iconic billionaires in the world—Warren Buffett.

Buffett grew up in a middle-class home. He actually didn't become the superrich billionaire who's a household symbol for wealth until he was in his fifties. So, how did he do it? How did a person born in Omaha, Nebraska, raised as a middle-class kid who attended public schools, become one of the wealthiest people on the planet? And an even better question—how did a person who grew up this way, who never invented anything life-changing or society-altering, end up one of the wealthiest people on the planet?

Usually, when we think of the wealthiest people, we think of entrepreneurs—people who started game-changing companies or culture-changing products. Steve Jobs founded Apple. Bill Gates started Microsoft. Mark Zuckerberg created Facebook. Elon Musk revolutionized electric cars with Tesla. But Warren Buffett? He didn't create anything new. The company he's most associated with—Berkshire Hathaway—can trace its beginnings back to the 1800s. So, what's the trick? How did he do it?

There's actually no magic trick to how Buffett built such immense wealth. All he did was what I'm teaching you to do: He always thought like a wealthy person and implemented a smart plan for building wealth over time. His plan was to be patient, to learn investing inside and out, and to apply that knowledge deliberately. Then he used that investing know-how to slowly make smart investments that accumulated wealth over many years. Because wise investments compound, the more money he invested, the faster his wealth grew. By the time he was in his fifties, he had amassed enough wealth that it compounded into an unbelievable fortune. It's like the old saying goes, "Money makes money." When it comes to investing and building wealth, the more you have, the more you make.

Think of it this way. Let's say there are two people investing in the same company: Person A invests one hundred dollars. Person B invests $100,000. If the value of this company doubles in a year's time, Person A now has $200. That's actually a great return on the investment. But Person

B, who made the same investment, now has $200,000. Same investment, same rate of return, but Person B made much more money.

Let's say both people keep all their investment in the company for a second year, and, again, the value doubles. Person A now has $400, and Person B has $400,000. If they both keep investing for two more years and the value continues to double each year, after four years, Person A has $1,600. Person B has $1,600,000. In other words, in four years, Person B became a millionaire. Money makes money.

That's the secret to Warren Buffett's long-term success. To be clear, money doesn't really make money this fast in the real world! I simplified this example greatly to illustrate the concept. Investing is a long-term process, and you must have a plan to do it over time.

But here's another thing about Warren Buffett: He was very patient, and he was an avid learner. He absorbed all he could about investing and learned about companies and markets. This knowledge gave him insight into how to leverage his money, and he was methodical in applying what he learned. He was methodical in the companies he chose to invest in, and he was methodical in timing those investments. Buffett wasn't just acting on a "gut feeling" or something he overheard. He didn't just invest thousands of dollars because he got a tip from a buddy.

No, he did his own research, and he always thought about the long term. He thought like a wealthy person, whereas so many people with a "rich mindset" want a lot of money right away. Those people look for short-term, quick-hit investments to make a lot of money in a short amount of time.

That's a losing proposition. Warren Buffett always invested in long-term returns. You should too.

But understanding your investments is critical. As I said, Buffett tried to learn everything he could about investing and markets—that's how he came to make his livelihood long before anyone called him the "Oracle of Omaha." That's not how most of us make a living, though. Most people are investing with a rich person's mindset, not a wealthy person's mindset. Buffett bases his decisions on research and understanding. He's not guessing, hoping, or praying. He's not taking random tips. He's taking action on what he knows.

I think that's a smart foundation for any wealth-building process. In my opinion, if I can't understand it, I shouldn't do it. If I can't explain what the investment is and how it works, I shouldn't act on it. If I don't know how a bond makes me money or how investing in a life insurance product builds cash value or how an annuity works, then those aren't things I should consider for my wealth-building process.

I've had lots of finance people say to me, "David, to build wealth, you've got to put your money in the market. You've got to buy a bond. You've got to get these annuities set up because these are the things that are going to make you wealthy." Well, they might be right that these vehicles can generate wealth, but if I don't understand them, I'd just be guessing and hoping. That's not tactical. It's not strategic. There's no real plan.

Here's the test if someone gives you investing advice: Ask them to explain how it works. If they can't explain it clearly, then they don't know either. For example, if a family member calls me and says, "David, I know you said you put your money in this thing. Can you tell me how it works?" and I start off with vague jargon that confuses them, then they'll know I'm full of crap. You should know that anyone who tries to hide behind complexity probably doesn't understand it well themselves.

Watch out for lines like:

- "Yeah, it's really complicated to explain. But I'll try."
- "I get it, but you should talk to your financial adviser who can explain it better."
- "This is very complex stuff. So I'll try to explain it, but I can't make any promises."
- "I'll give you the brief version, and then you can talk to my adviser for the details."

These are all BS lines. Don't let anyone make you feel stupid. If someone truly understands something, they should be able to explain it in simple terms. If they can't, they don't get it themselves—and if you also don't understand it, that's the blind leading the blind. As I've said before, that's not a strategy for building generational wealth.

The way I see it, you need to fully understand any investment before you commit to it. That's why I like real estate. With real estate, you can see it, you can touch it, and it's easier to understand. Most people will buy a house at some point, and they know that, usually, the house appreciates in value over time. With each mortgage payment, you build more equity, generating cash flow and enjoying tax savings. It's straightforward, which is why I recommend real estate as a first investment strategy for many people. Building wealth is about understanding what you're doing and then using your money to do it.

Take Control of Your Investments

Here's the thing: Many people are content with the "blind leading the blind" approach to building wealth. Why? Because there's a strong narrative that says we're all too dumb to understand finance and investment strategy. It suggests that these investment vehicles are so complex that only a so-called "expert" can really understand them.

The second part of this narrative is that you shouldn't bother trying. You're supposed to hand over control of your savings, your money, and your financial future to someone else—someone who supposedly knows better. So strong is this narrative that even really smart people follow it without question, trusting strangers with their entire financial futures.

It's kind of crazy when you think about it. The narrative says that doing it yourself isn't the right way. Instead, you should rely on a financial adviser or a certain type of account or let your employer handle everything. Basically, it says anyone but you should manage your money.

Don't just blindly follow this narrative. It's your money, and it can shape your entire life. Don't cede all control of your financial future. Take control of it! Be an active participant in creating your own wealth. Yes, having passive income is great, but you don't create wealth passively; you create wealth actively, just like you create anything worthwhile in life.

There's no such thing as a meaningful passive activity. Strong relationships, successful careers, lasting health—all require active involvement. The same is true for building wealth. Even if you think real estate investing is "passive," you're still actively managing aspects of it: property managers, bank accounts, expenses, maintenance.

So, when considering your wealth-generation process, ask yourself: Am I going to be passive, or am I going to be active? If you're passive, you'll never have true control. If you're active—like Warren Buffett—you question, you learn, you take responsibility. You meet with advisers and ask, "Where would you put my money and why?" You dig into risks and rewards. Being active means you're intentional; you're in the driver's seat.

The myth persists that understanding finances requires some special genius, but Warren Buffett himself often says investing is simple math: addition, subtraction, multiplication, division. It took me years to break free from the myth that it was more complicated than that. Once I did, everything became clear and easier. That's what we're going to do for you as we move forward.

But you can't do this unless you're ready to take control. I like to think of it in terms of driving. I love driving myself everywhere because I control the route, the timing, the speed. If I make a mistake, I learn from it. If I let someone else drive all the time, I learn nothing and control nothing.

The same goes for creating generational wealth. The more control you have, the more responsibility you take. The more responsibility you take, the more you learn and understand. And the more you learn and understand, the more wealth you generate over time.

Vehicles of Wealth Building

Knowing what you're investing in is the first step. Taking control of that process is the second. The third piece is knowing exactly what to learn about and what to take control of. Let's talk about the different vehicles for building wealth.

You can't build wealth without money. As we said, "Money makes money." We've already discussed my preferred vehicle, real estate, so let's explore others.

Of course, you can simply save money bit by bit. Saving a dollar a day yields $365 in a year. That's a good start, but obviously, if you save more per day, you'll have more to leverage for future investments. The more you save, the faster your wealth can grow.

Let's say you want to buy Apple stock at $365 a share. If you save a dollar a day, after a year, you can buy one share. If Apple goes up 10 percent, you earn about $36.50. That's a great return, but with so little invested, the gain is tiny in absolute terms. To really leverage returns, you need more money to invest. Fundamentally, you need to generate more income before investing can really accelerate your wealth.

This is a critical point. Most people don't earn millions a year. They have a decent income, but it's limited. The more money you make, the more you can leverage, and the easier it becomes to generate wealth. That's why high-earning employees or entrepreneurs have a distinct advantage.

Be Your Own Boss

Another powerful vehicle for wealth generation is becoming your own boss. When you're your own boss, your income isn't capped by a company's pay structure. You have opportunities to expand, scale, and create multiple income streams.

If you make $50,000 as an employee now, you could branch out on your own, freelance, or start an online business. As you gain clients or customers, you might double that income, add employees, and keep scaling up. It's not easy—entrepreneurship is challenging and not for everyone—but if your goal is to build wealth, being an entrepreneur can be the number one vehicle to get you there.

Invest in Industries You Work In

As we discussed, understanding what you invest in is key. This often means looking at markets or industries you're already familiar with. For me, I'm in the accounting and tax industry, so if I were to invest in something related to accounting, I'd already have an advantage because I understand it well.

If you're in construction, consider construction-related investments. If you run a salon, look at beauty industry products or services. Whatever your field—energy, tech, health care—your insider knowledge helps you identify promising opportunities that others might overlook.

Side note: Even as an employee, you might consider investing in your employer, if possible. You have unique insights about whether the company is on an upward trajectory. Maybe you can receive stock instead of a raise or convert bonuses into equity. Ask if the company welcomes investors. Because you understand the business from the inside, you're making an informed decision.

Look for Base Hits, Not Home Runs

Keeping with the mantra of "know what you're investing in," it's easier to research something you're already familiar with or enjoy. Warren Buffett famously says never invest in a company whose product you don't use. He looks for companies that never go out of style—like Coca-Cola. He doesn't look for something that rockets from zero to a hundred overnight because what shoots up that fast can also crash just as quickly.

Look for investments that grow steadily. If you understand that wealth generation requires patience and strategy, you'll realize that consistent base hits are often better than swinging for a home run every time. You can hit more base hits than home runs, which leads to more stable growth over the long term.

This takes discipline and self-control because there's always someone pitching a "get rich quick" scheme. That's when you have to remember to think wealthy, not rich. Know that you're playing the long game. Stay focused on building generational wealth.

By understanding what you're investing in, taking control of your investments, and selecting the right vehicles for growth, you'll be well on your way to building lasting wealth. In the chapters ahead, we'll continue refining your strategies, helping you create a realistic, long-term plan that supports not just you, but the future generations who will benefit from your wise decisions today.

Chapter 3: The Process of Building Wealth

Wealth Reflections

1. What investments have you made without truly understanding them, and how will you approach them differently now?

2. How could becoming more actively involved in your investments increase your confidence and control over your financial future?

3. Which steps can you take this month to become more intentional and strategic in your wealth-building process?

4

WHERE ARE YOU STARTING FROM?

In the last chapter, we established the process for investing to build wealth. But before you put that process into action, there's a crucial step we need to address. Ironically, it's a commonsense step that most people never think much about. That is, on your journey to building wealth, the first thing you need to do is know where you're starting from.

Here's the thing: knowing where you want to end up is easy. And that goes for anything in life. Everyone wants to make money. Hell, everyone wants to make a lot of money. Everyone wants to be a millionaire. Everyone wants to save money. Everyone wants to be good-looking, have six-pack abs, travel the world. In short, everyone wants to be better than what they are or what they have today. So the end point is easy. It's the getting there that's really hard.

Every journey starts somewhere. But most people don't stop to think about where they're starting from. And if you don't know where you're starting from, how do you know how to get to your destination?

Let's think about this in everyday terms. When you're visiting a new city and you want to go someplace—say, a restaurant for dinner—you find one you like and map it on your phone. The very next question the GPS asks you is, "Is this your current location?" Why? Because it's impossible for the GPS to plot a route to your destination without knowing where you're starting from.

The same goes for you in anything you want to achieve. You can't plot an effective path to reach your goals without knowing where you're starting from. The path to getting six-pack abs, for example, for a person who has been exercising and watching what they eat their whole life is much different from that of a person who has never seen the inside of a gym and is inclined to overindulge in sweets and fatty foods.

The same goes for becoming a millionaire. The path to becoming a millionaire for a person who makes six figures, owns a half-million-dollar home, and has a lot of money saved is much different from the path for a person who is an employee, rents a one-bedroom apartment, and is living pay-check to paycheck. Both people can absolutely get to where they want to go, but the paths they take and the strategies they use along the way are different.

Be Honest with Yourself

Any plan for building generational wealth is predicated on where you are starting from. To know your starting point requires you to be very honest. You need to be very, very honest with yourself. The hardest part about doing anything in life is just being honest about it. I know this because for a long time I wasn't honest with myself.

When I first started out and was losing money in my companies, I wasn't necessarily being the best steward of my finances. I, for example, used my business account to pay for my personal stuff. After a while, I did it without thinking. Taking money from the business became a habit—a very bad and expensive habit—and it made accurate accounting of both my business and my personal finances impossible.

When things started crumbling around me, I had to be honest. I had to say, Dude, you can't use the business card to do personal things. You can't just take money out when you need it. You can't go to the ATM like it's giving out free candy. You need to stop doing these things because, if you don't, you're going to lose everything.

When I decided to make that shift, it wasn't because I thought, I'm better than that. It was more like, Okay, be honest with yourself. Is this the way to run your companies? To run your life? No. So, what are you going to do about it? You've got to do something here, because if you don't do something different, the outcome is not going to be good. It's not going to be what I want.

The thing is, if I wasn't honest with myself, I wouldn't have been able to make the changes I needed to make. The same goes for you. We can't fix what we don't know is broken. In fact, a lot of times, we may know something is broken, but we don't want to admit it. If you have bad spending habits, if you have bad money management habits, if you don't know how much money you have in your bank account, if you don't know how much money you need to pay your bills, if you don't have any idea what your discretionary spending looks like, then guess what? You can't start doing anything constructive. You can't fix anything. You can't chart a path to building wealth because you have no idea where you are, where you're starting from.

Sure, you can try to wing it. You can just jump right in and create a big plan for generating and building wealth. But you will invariably find yourself lost. You'll find that you're not making any progress. Why? Because how would you even know what "progress" is if you don't know where you started from in the first place?

And if you didn't have the discipline to sit down and be honest with yourself about your flaws, your finances, and your income—everything—there's no chance you'll have the discipline to follow through with long-term, wealth-building plans that require far more time and energy to execute. It all starts with knowing where you are right now—and being brutally honest about that starting place.

Start with Your Tax Return

Once you commit to being honest with yourself, what's the next step? I like to think about taxes as a good starting point. It's something that no one wants to think about but that you absolutely must think about! And I don't mean just paying taxes; I mean filing a tax return. Filing a tax return annually is a requirement of every taxpayer, or income earner, in this country, as it is in most countries. So looking at your tax return gives you the hard numbers about what money you made in the last year. Then, ask yourself, How much of that do I actually still have? What's left here?

It might seem like this should be fairly straightforward, but it's not. Some people, for example, have very large incomes. I've filed returns for people who make a million dollars a year. And then I ask them, "How much do you actually have in cash in the bank?" And they might say, "Ten grand."

This, again, is the rich person's mindset, and as we've discussed, it's a very easy mindset to fall into. It's easy to look from the outside in and say, "Oh, people like that are so stupid. That would never be me. Never. If I was making a million dollars, I would have so much money, I would just save all the time. I'd stockpile tons of cash."

I'm here to tell you that the chances are, you wouldn't. It's incredibly easy to get swept up in the rich lifestyle. You're surrounded by nice things and people constantly talking about money and spending money and living the life that everyone always dreams about. And if you have money, believe me, you'll start spending it too. And you'll feel financially secure because you have so much income every week, every month. It's easy to just keep spending. Until one day, you realize you don't have anything to show for it.

That's rich living, which is easy. Wealthy living is far more challenging. You have to be intentional. You have to be disciplined. And that's why looking at that tax return and checking it against how much you have left is a great starting point.

So let's start there—with a simple tax return. You can do your own personal audit. Ask yourself, How much do I have in my bank account after the end of the year, how much went to investments, and how much went to discretionary lifestyle spending? And by lifestyle spending, I mean how much did you spend on personal travel, eating out, leisure and entertainment, and the like. Really drill down here and do your own profit and loss assessment. But when you do this, leave out your business. This should be about your own personal life—knowing how many bills come in, how much money goes out for bills, what's left at the end of the month, how much you pay to investments, what you do with the money, where your biggest expenses are.

And let me be clear, this is something you should absolutely do to get a sense of your starting point, but this is also something we all need to do periodically. I suggest my clients do this monthly. Doing it once a year is not enough because we all lead busy lives, and these types of personal expenses can slip away from us despite our best intentions. A few months ago, my bookkeeper was allocating expenses for me on a monthly basis for my personal life. And he bundled some monthly expenses together under the category "Communications," which included internet, phone, and some other items. Much to my surprise, it was coming out to $800 a month! I was like, whoa! How did this happen?

So I started digging into the numbers. I saw that one of the expenses was for cable TV, which was a shock because I don't even watch cable anymore. But I had neglected that. The cable bill itself wasn't huge, but it's not even something I use.

And this is the way it happens. These little bills add up to a lot of money. Companies actually count on us not being able to keep track of these things. That cable bill, for example, started with a promotion when I first set up the system, and then I just forgot about it. The same goes for all the streaming platforms now. There are dozens of streaming platforms to choose from. All of them have nominal monthly charges—ten dollars, twenty dollars—but people now have subscriptions to platforms they don't even use, that they don't even know they have.

All those subscriptions add up and chip away at our savings, which, ultimately, chips away at the wealth we're trying to build. So it's important to dig into all these things, to know your expenses from top to bottom.

Be Your Business

Basically, by starting with your tax return and doing a personal audit, you begin to run your personal life like a business. And if we run our lives like a business, then we have the ability to make better decisions and chart a clearer path to our destination, which is wealth. Let's go further into this by digging into the details of what a personal profit and loss statement looks like.

Every month, you should be reconciling your expenses against your income, and you should be scrutinizing it, as I recently had to do with my communications bill. Once I realized that the umbrella category "Communications" was actually obscuring my ability to properly evaluate my monthly costs, I told my bookkeeper to break down that category into individual items—phone, internet, cable, and so forth—so I could clearly see, and then clearly assess, each item and whether the cost was acceptable or not.

This is what a business would do, and so this is what you should be doing to better run your personal life as a business would. Because a thriving business must be profitable. And you can't be a profitable business if your costs exceed your revenue. In our personal lives, this means our expenses can't exceed our income. After all, the most important vehicle to wealth creation is you. If the business of yourself is not in order, it won't matter what else you're doing or investing in. You'll never get to where you want to be.

Every day we spend working and pushing to make money and to do better for our families is an investment. It's an investment of time, and your time is exchanged for something in return, which we call money. When we get the money, what we do with that money is our decision. We have the ability to make that decision every day. Where our money goes is ultimately up to us, and how much we make is ultimately up to us as well.

But at the end of the month, what's left over is also a result of what we decided to do with our money, and if we don't know what we decided to do with our money on a monthly basis, then our business is obviously not going to grow and expand the way it should. The best case is that we maintain the status quo, just survive from month to month. More likely is that, over time, the business declines. It will lose money and go deeper into debt. Businesses, like people, don't thrive under mountains of debt.

Think about it this way. Say you were going to invest in a business today, and you wanted to do some firsthand research by talking to the owners. And you ask, "Can you tell me what your primary expenses are?" And they reply with something like, "Let's see, we spend on marketing, and we have to pay rent and utilities, and we obviously have employee salaries to pay, and we have a bunch of vendors we pay monthly. We're missing stuff, for sure, but you get the picture. We have a lot of bills."

Then you follow up by asking, "How much are the bills, and what percentage are they of your monthly overhead costs?" And they say, "Well, it varies. Depends on the month. Sometimes it's more and sometimes it's less. We're not really sure offhand."

Finally, after getting these wishy-washy answers, you ask, "How much do you usually make on a monthly basis?" And, again, they're like, "Well, it varies. Sometimes we make this, sometimes we make that. It depends on the month and what's going on."

How confident would you be investing in that business when the owners don't seem to have a clear idea of what their fixed expenditures are versus what kind of revenue they're bringing in?

Compare a business like that to one where you ask the same questions, and the owners provide much more direct answers.

"How much money did you make last month?"

"We made $13,227."

"Is that a typical profit for your business?"

"No, the month before that we made $16,000, and the month before that we made $12,000."

"How do you account for such variable profits?"

"Because some months we have more supply orders. In fact, last month, we ordered $4,000 more in supplies, which brought down our profit margin and impacted our bottom line. But we know this typically needs to happen quarterly, so it prompts us to make different decisions."

What I'm getting at in this example is this: You would have far more trust and confidence in the second business than in the first. Anyone would. Why? Because they know their business. They know the numbers. And if you know where your money goes at all times, then you always can tell yourself what you should be doing with your money, how you can invest your money, where it should go, and how it should be spent. And you make better decisions investing.

So let's take this full circle. Let's say you are the business. If somebody was going to invest in you, could you give them good information? Could you detail all your finances? After all, like any business, you're investing in you every day. Could you provide clear, concise answers to an investor's questions? It's a very illuminating way to see yourself as an investible asset, a business, because you are.

Conduct a Wealth Assessment

Ultimately, to know where you're starting from, you need to know your financial health. Your financial health is a broader picture of where you are as it relates to savings, investments, and taxes. To do this, my company would conduct what we call a wealth assessment, from which we establish a financial goal—what we call a Financial Freedom Target—which details where you want to be in dollars so that you can live the life you want.

By looking at your income, investments, and taxes, we have a sense of where you're starting from, which then helps us establish the target. Because if you don't have a target, none of this matters. If you don't know how much money you're going to need or what you're going to do, you're lost. As I've been saying, this all starts by looking at where you're starting from.

Let's say, for example, our client James is making $100,000 a year. We'd say, "Do you feel like that amount can continue to deliver the same quality of life that you would want?" Oftentimes, people don't know, which is why they're coming to us for help and guidance. Let's say James isn't sure.

We then ask him a series of questions to try to figure out how much he thinks he will need to live the life he wants without working. Once we establish that number, say it is $200,000 a year, we then set a target date, the Financial Freedom Date, which is the date James wants to be free of work obligations—the date he is essentially free to live exactly how he wants. That means James can continue working if he chooses, but he won't have to because he'll have built enough wealth to be free of work constraints. Now, let's say James says twenty years. This means James has twenty years to make it, to have $200,000 a year coming in without having to do anything.

The next thing we do is look at investments. We look at their performance over time to forecast what they would be generating in twenty years. We can look at an investment's performance history and make projections on that annualized yield. Once we know what those investment sums would look like in twenty years, we can produce an annualized distribution amount. An annualized distribution is how much money James can take out of that account every year without affecting the actual balance. Let's say we set it at 5 percent. Then that would give us the income figure, which may be close to

$200,000, or it might not. It depends on how much savings James is projected to have by his Financial Freedom Date.

As another example, let's say you had $1 million in total savings, and you're at your Financial Freedom Date and ready to start taking out your 5 percent annualized distribution. And let's say your savings are accruing 8 percent interest year over year. That would be roughly $80,000 a year that you could take out. So every year, whatever you invested in, it's going to make $80,000 because you have this million dollars in principal. But we're going to take out only 5 percent, which is $50,000. This leaves 3 percent interest still growing year over year. We do this because this accounts for the annual benchmark inflation rate, which is 3 percent. We don't take out all the interest—in this case, 8 percent—so that your money continues to grow while you're living off it.

At an 8 percent interest rate on $1 million in total savings, you could be living on $50,000 a year, without touching the principal. But that's not enough for our client James, who wants to be living on $200,000 a year. James, then, would have to have $4 million in total savings to have $200,000 at a 5 percent annualized distribution.

So we have to create a plan that would get James to save $4 million within twenty years. That's why it is so critical to understand where you're starting from. Starting at zero dollars in savings requires a far different plan than starting at $150,000 in savings.

Typically, the next thing we do is check taxes. We look to see whether James is overpaying in taxes. That's the first place we can reallocate money from that James already has but is currently wasting. Money saved in taxes is then money applied to savings.

This is the general process of a wealth assessment. First, know where we're starting from. Then, figure out where we want to be. Next, we build a plan to achieve the Financial Freedom Target goal by the Financial Freedom Date. When all is said and done, it boils down to simple math. For example, We've got to save X amount of money in Y amount of time to achieve James's Financial Freedom Target.

It's a very common and simple formula; however, most people don't take into account the tax liability aspect. There are the current taxes a person is paying, but then there are also the taxes they'll pay when they take money out of their investments, which need to be accounted for as well—and which almost no one ever considers, even though the amount can be substantial. We create a plan for tax liability; that is, we figure out which strategies we need to put in place to lower overall tax liability in both the short term and the long term.

Often, that involves investing in something. It could be real estate, it could be energy, it could be a retirement vehicle, it could be a business. Once we establish the vehicles for wealth generation, we set annual investment amounts for each. We make our clients commit to the plan. It's nonnegotiable. We do this because we know that most high performers—most people in general, actually—are too busy to plan this all out, to think this critically about their long-term financial future. Creating a systematic plan that they must follow over the years is the only way to achieve their goals.

Chapter 4: Where Are You Starting From?

Wealth Reflections

1. When was the last time you took an honest look at your finances, and what did you learn from that experience?

2. What fears arise when you confront your current financial position, and how might facing them help you grow?

3. How would having a clear starting point influence your long-term wealth strategy?

5

INVESTMENTS AND TAX PLANNING—
THE WEALTHY COMBINATION

In the last chapter, we focused on the often-overlooked step of taking the time to know where you're starting from in relation to your wealth-building plan. In this chapter, let's talk about another frequent wealth-building blunder: Most people know vaguely that they need to "invest" but very few think about a plan for managing taxes. Big mistake. Very big.

Both taxes and investments play vital roles and are equally important in building generational wealth. But if we tackle one and not the other, we're not going to build wealth successfully. I understood this early in my career. I purchased my first real estate investment property in 2011 for $65,000. It was the largest investment I'd made in my life. It was a foreclosed commercial property. I didn't have much money, but the bank was desperate to get rid of it. They let me have it for 10 percent down. Funny thing, I barely had even that much money to put down. I didn't know what I was getting myself into, but I knew this was the right move. My tax business needed a new office, and I wanted to rent this space to my business. It would be a win-win!

So that's what I did: I rented the space to my business for double the cost of my mortgage. It was great! I was making cash flow. This was the first time in my life that I felt rich (not at all wealthy yet). True to rich form, that year I bought a new car and upgraded my lifestyle. Things were good.

But at that time, I wasn't yet tax-savvy. The only thing I understood about taxes was that I needed to file tax returns. That year, I added my new building to my tax return and filed my taxes as usual. That was it. Looking back, however, I realize I did it all wrong. Even though the investment was good, I missed out on immediate tax savings. I'd say I lost at least $20,000 that year because I did not plan out my taxes and file properly.

The sneaky thing about taxes is that you don't know what you don't know. Had I not come to understand tax planning as I do now, I would not think anything of that time period. As I said, nothing "bad" happened, and it was still a pivotal year for me in that I purchased my first investment property. The IRS never came knocking on my door because I did something "wrong." The thing is, I didn't do it right. I only knew half the equation. I knew real estate investment—I didn't know tax strategy. And that lack of knowledge cost me $20,000!

Once you understand the two parts—investments and taxes—you start making wealthy decisions and avoid missed opportunities. That's how you build generational wealth. This chapter will show you how to do it.

Three Primary Investment Tracks

There's a lot more to investing today than just getting a return on investment (ROI). To build real wealth, you need a clear plan and a full understanding of your options because without proper understanding, it can be dizzying. In fact, there's so much information out there, with so many different investment vehicles being pitched all the time, that it can be downright paralyzing. Let's simplify things.

We can reduce all this down to three primary investment options.

Number one, you can do nothing—just the bare minimum. As discussed in chapter 3, the people in this first group who choose to do the minimum are the ones who don't take control of their investments and financial future. Instead, they cede their authority over their earnings to someone else. They put their money in a savings account or pay a financial adviser to put it into a passive index fund. This is conventional thinking. It's safe, sure, but it's not going to generate the kind of wealth you're seeking over the long term.

Then there's the second option. This group invests in anything to make money. And when I say anything, I mean anything! They're ROI hogs. They'll do whatever they can to maximize return. They might put their money in Bitcoin, invest based on a stock tip from a friend or a podcast, or jump headfirst into the latest trending meme stock. If they could make money flipping horses or cows, they'd do it. They're not risk averse at all—in fact, you could argue they're recklessly risky. They're not investing with their heads; they're investing with their heart or gut or just a desire to get rich fast. Some might get rich, but unless they're extremely lucky, none will be truly wealthy. They're the epitome of the rich mindset, not the wealthy mindset. They're primed for the rich trap.

Finally, there's the third group—people whose investment strategy allows them to get both tax benefits and ROI. At my firm, we call this the 3 Percent Club. Why 3 percent? Because people who actively engage in both investing and tax planning to build true generational wealth are rare, just like those who actually achieve true generational wealth are rare. I estimate it at about 3 percent of the population. These people are intentional in their financial planning. They scrutinize the tax side as much as the investment side. In planning for both, they accumulate real wealth.

Addition by Reduction: The Time Value of Money

Building wealth depends heavily on how we keep and grow our money. The biggest expense you'll have in life is taxes. Taxes are estimated to take 40 to 50 percent of your income over your lifetime. That's a lot, right? For most, it's higher than they think. There's federal income tax, state income tax, local and sales taxes, real estate and property taxes, registration and vehicle taxes, estate taxes—it's endless. And that's just what you pay out. Most people don't consider the opportunity cost of those payouts.

Think of it this way: Every dollar paid in taxes is a lost opportunity for investment capital. You can't make money on money you don't have. Investments are the vehicle that fuels your income. The more fuel (money) you have, the farther you can go. If you're continuously paying too much in taxes, you're depleting the fuel you need to achieve your financial goals. Creating a wealth generation plan by focusing only on investments but ignoring taxes is like driving to a distant destination with a leak in your gas tank. You'll run out of fuel before you arrive!

This is why tax planning is so important. With good tax planning, you gain money by not losing it unnecessarily. It's addition by reduction. By reducing taxes, you add fuel to your investment vehicles, generating more returns. This ties back to the time value of money. You want to generate more money in a shorter amount of time, but you can't do that if you're hemorrhaging cash to taxes. If I'd rather have $100,000 today than $10,000 each year for ten years, it's because having the money sooner lets me invest and grow it faster. In terms of taxes, I want to retain as much as possible now to maximize my ROI over time.

Let's revisit that $20,000 I paid in taxes years ago when I didn't need to. Nothing "bad" happened then—no IRS trouble, and I'd made an important investment. But in terms of wealth building, it was a huge loss. Let's do a conservative calculation: If I had saved that $20,000 and invested it at 5 percent interest (a very modest return), after some years, I'd have tens of thousands more. Over decades, it could become $140,000 or more. By not planning my taxes properly, I lost out on about $150,000 of potential wealth—wealth that would have kept compounding over time.

This is why tax planning is critical. It prevents lost opportunities and accelerates your wealth generation.

Long-Term Investing and Short-Term Tax Planning

You often hear about long-term and short-term investments. Knowing the difference matters. Applying the same concept to your tax planning is also crucial. I advise my clients: Think long-term for investments and short-term for tax planning.

Long-Term Investing

As we discussed, people with a rich mindset want quick returns. They're not patient. But real investing—investing for generational wealth—is long term. There's no such thing as ATM investing, where you put in money and out comes more money instantly. Real investing means putting in money and waiting years for it to grow. It means thinking strategically and patiently.

For example, I have a real estate fund. I'm selective about who invests because if you're not a long-term investor, you're not really investing—you're just gambling. We're building communities that take years to develop. Any investor must be comfortable with a long and uncertain horizon—seven, ten, fifteen years—before seeing big returns. That's real wealth-building investing.

Immediate returns come from work, from deploying your skills. Investing should be about long-term growth. Wealth generation understands that money isn't scarce; you can always earn more using your skills. The investments are there to grow what you save, not to provide instant gratification.

Short-Term Tax Planning

In contrast, tax planning should be considered on a shorter term—say five years or fewer. Income and laws can change, so planning too far out doesn't help as much. Five years is a reasonable time frame to estimate income and strategize tax savings.

A great example is how the tax code can favor corporations after five years. If I build a corporation, after five years, I might qualify for a $10 million tax-free capital gains exclusion when I sell it. Knowing this up-front means I plan to hold that company for at least five years to reap huge tax savings. Selling too soon would be a costly blunder. By understanding these rules, I can retain more money to fuel investments that grow my wealth even more.

Treat Your Taxes as You Should Your Health

Think of tax planning like health. Everyone wants to be healthy, but most people only treat symptoms as they appear. That's traditional medicine. Functional medicine looks for root causes to prevent problems before they occur.

The same goes for taxes. Traditional tax thinking is reactive—after the transaction, after the year is over. Functional tax planning addresses the root issues up-front, so you're not just reacting to tax bills after they hit. By proactively reducing tax burdens at the source, you keep more money that can compound and grow your investments over time.

Just like a persistent headache might be a sign of a bigger health issue, paying too much in taxes is a sign of a bigger financial issue—lack of proactive planning. Solve the root cause, and you'll be healthier financially. Fix your tax strategy, and you free up money to invest, accelerating your path to generational wealth.

By understanding that both investments and tax planning must work hand in hand, you ensure you're not just building wealth but protecting and growing it efficiently. In the next chapters, we'll continue to refine these strategies, ensuring you have the tools to maximize every dollar and achieve the long-term financial freedom you've been working toward.

Chapter 5: Investments and Tax Planning— The Wealthy Combination

Wealth Reflections

1. How might understanding tax strategy open new investment opportunities you've never considered before?

2. In what ways might you be losing "fuel" (money) through unnecessary taxes, and how can you fix that?

3. Which small but immediate steps can you take to better integrate tax planning with your investment approach?

6

HOW TO KEEP YOUR MONEY—
TAX STRATEGY EXPLAINED

In the last chapter, I explained the importance of tax planning. Just as much as smart investments, tax planning is critical to building generational wealth. In this chapter, we will dig into exactly how you go about optimizing your taxes so that you keep as much of your money as possible to fuel your investment vehicles.

I stress your money here because it's important, first and foremost, to understand that this isn't in any way a plan to "short" or "stiff" the government. We're almost brainwashed to think that taxes are the government's money. But that's nonsense. It literally makes no sense. The government gets all its money from us, individual citizens like you and me. We earn the money and then, through tax law, we give some of that money to the government to be used for the public good. We have to trust that the people we elect will spend our money wisely.

I remember reading back in 2005 how the government was spending fifty dollars for a roll of toilet paper and thinking to myself, That isn't right. Yet, that's just how it is. Like it or not, the government isn't incentivized to be a good steward of our tax dollars. This is exactly why we must work to find ways to keep more of our hard-earned money.

What good could you do if you kept another 10 percent of your earned income?

Let's discuss why most people pay taxes blindly and believe that it's just the way it has to be.

Part of the disconnect comes in how taxes are collected. For most W-2 employees, for example, taxes are taken out of paychecks beforehand—that is, the employee receives what remains after the government takes its cut. This process of automatically withholding taxes dates back to the 1940s. As the country geared up for war against Japan and Germany in World War II, the government enacted automatic tax withholding to expedite collections when the nation needed funds fast. Even after the war ended, this process continued. Property taxes work much the same way. Many homeowners roll taxes and mortgage payments into an escrow account, paying them automatically each month.

My point is that most people don't literally pay out their taxes to the government each month or quarter. It all just happens by default, without them doing anything. I'm not saying there's anything wrong with that process. In many ways, it makes life simpler for workers and homeowners. Most people accept it as "the way it is," which is fine. But the downside is that we've lost a sense of ownership of what's rightfully ours. The taxes federal and state agencies collect consist of our money. The money you pay in taxes is your money. Keep this top of mind as you read this chapter.

Playing the Tax Game

The tax code is actually a game, and I can help you understand how to master it. But to master any game—to win—you have to know the rules. To excel at any game, you need a strategy.

"Those Who Know the Rules Rule!"

All great players don't just show up; they practice, study their opponents, and prepare meticulously. Tom Brady didn't become the greatest quarterback of all time on pure talent alone. Football is a team sport that demands enormous scheming, strategizing, and scrutinizing of each opponent. Brady spent endless hours studying game tapes, learning his opponents' schemes, players, tendencies, and weaknesses. Without understanding every last detail each week, he wouldn't have achieved his remarkable success. Preparation and knowledge set him apart. We're going to take the same approach in our tax game.

For our purposes, think of the IRS as your opponent. We'll study it. We'll watch the "tapes," so to speak. By studying the IRS, we'll know where to attack, just like Tom Brady did with his opponents. Most people fear the IRS, but what they don't realize is that IRS agents reviewing your returns aren't as well-versed in the code as you might think. The IRS faces challenges like any big organization—training people on a complex code in a short period, dealing with massive workloads, and being overstretched. This leaves room for error on their part and gives a competitive advantage to someone who understands the code well.

The takeaway is that you should stop seeing the IRS as an invincible giant. Being intimidated essentially guarantees defeat. If you view the IRS instead as an overworked, under-staffed team prone to mistakes, you'll realize they are far from unbeatable.

So, let's get to it!

My Biggest Tax Blunder

It all started in 2013. By then, my business was growing at the speed I wanted. I had the mindset "more equals more." More customers, employees, offices—that meant more success to me. So in 2013, I committed to expanding the business no matter what.

In the tax preparation business, that's how you grow. We weren't a traditional CPA firm doing bookkeeping and accounting. We were churning out tax returns like an H&R Block—simple, scalable service for everyday people who just needed to file before a deadline. No complex specialization required. In 2013, I had five offices. Over the next two years, I kept opening office after office.

A local competitor had fourteen offices. To beat them, I wanted fifteen. I had no real plan, just knew I needed money. I found a lender who gave me $1 million at 12 percent for sixteen months. I was hungry and agreed to the terms.

With that $1 million, I basically had two tax seasons to pay it back. I was all in: finding locations, negotiating leases, even going to Walmart and Family Dollar stores to open offices wherever possible. I opened ten new offices in under twelve months, totaling fifteen—one more than my competitor.

I set up signage, offices, hired staff—if you were breathing, I'd hire you. I worked tirelessly to expand quickly.

By the end of the second tax season, I realized I wouldn't hit my projections. I turned $1 million into just over $1 million, not the $2.5 million I planned. I was short, nearly out of money. The bank called, wanting to settle up. I panicked.

I called the bank and said, "I'll pay you, but not all now. After settling some debts, I'll file bankruptcy." The bank said they'd bury me.

I had a mentor, a retired banker and CPA, who offered help. Scared and desperate, I accepted. He helped me negotiate a deal to pay off the debt over two years and keep some cash. I thought I was in the clear—little did I know what was coming.

Tax season arrived. I filed my return. On the second page of the 1040, it said, "You owe $142,000." I nearly lost my mind. I had no money, made no money, was drowning in debt. How could I owe $142,000?!

I spent the night combing through the tax code, looking for a way out. I realized you can't write off loan repayments. My financial reality meant nothing to the IRS. Again, I didn't know what I was doing with taxes—this was the difference between being a tax preparer and a tax strategist. I had to report all the income paid back to the bank, counting against me for taxes, and now I had to figure out how to pay that $142,000.

In a panic, I went to my mentor. He confirmed I owed it. I ranted: "There's got to be a way! The Warren Buffetts, Bill Gateses, and Trumps of the world don't pay like this. They have work-arounds!" After going on for minutes, I finally stopped. He calmly said, "There's no other way. You have to pay."

At my lowest moment, I vowed never to be in that position again. I learned two huge lessons: (1) I'd never go into reckless debt again—more isn't always more. (2) Paying taxes was a symptom of not planning properly, of not having a real strategy. From now on, I'd find ways to lower my taxes and never be stuck like that again.

The Tax Code: The Rules of the Tax Game

As I said, taxes are a game. Most lose because the rules (the tax code) are complicated. If you don't understand the rules, you'll lose. The tax code is around 6,900 pages—five times longer than *War and Peace*. Add guides and regulations, and it's over 70,000 pages. Nobody reads it all, and who benefits from that? Not you.

Yes, it's a game. The IRS is your opponent, the tax code, the rule book. You must crack the code. But how can you if it's too long and dense? That's where I come in. Like any game, there are cheat codes or hacks. Certain strategies work best in certain situations.

To be clear, these cheat codes aren't illegal. We're playing by the rules they wrote. We're not breaking or bending laws. We're simply using their vulnerabilities—the loopholes—in our favor, so we start winning rather than losing.

Not All Income Is Created Equal (Because It's Not Taxed Equally)

We pay income tax, but not all income is equal. Earned income (a job or paid employment) is taxed highest—up to 37 percent federally, plus more at the state level. Passive income from investments is taxed lower. Warren Buffett pays a lower percentage than his secretary because he earns through investments, and she earns through labor. The tax code favors investors, not workers.

There are short-term and long-term capital gains. Short-term gains are taxed like regular income. Long-term gains are much lower (15 or 20 percent). For someone earning $500,000, their labor income might be taxed at 35 percent but their investments at 20 percent. That's why executives take compensation as stock options—to save huge amounts over time.

How you get paid determines your tax. To be strategic, find ways to receive dollars at the lowest effective tax rate.

Tax Structures to Optimize Earnings (and Reduce Tax Burdens)

Your tax strategy starts with understanding your income sources. Different strategies apply to different situations.

If you're a business owner, the structure you pick—sole proprietorship, S corporation, C corporation, partnership, limited liability company (LLC)—affects taxes. The government ensures it gets Social Security and Medicare from you. Either you take a paycheck (W-2) or pay self-employment taxes at filing.

For my clients, we often choose W-2 income through a corporate structure. This avoids the full 15 percent self-employment tax. As a W-2 employee, you pay half, and the corporation pays half.

Many new business owners pick LLCs or sole props—easier but not tax-advantageous. LLCs are about liability, not tax. S corps, however, are recognized as corporate entities, taxed on profits, and can pay the owner a W-2 wage, giving more control and flexibility.

Invest to Zero, Don't Expense to Zero

Tax strategies depend on how big your tax bill is. Tax-favored investments can lower it. If you owe $25,000, you can find write-offs—equipment, machinery, vehicles—to reduce that burden.

No single move erases all taxes. Smart strategy chips away at the burden incrementally. Each retained dollar fuels your investments and compounds over time.

If your tax bill is $500,000 and you use multiple strategies, maybe you save $50,000 to $100,000. That's huge over decades. But maybe you still owe $400,000 and want to lower it further—then you invest in oil, gas, real estate, defined benefit plans, charitable finance. If your liability is $50,000 or more, consider a serious investment strategy for tax reduction.

People often think they can just expense everything to zero. But if you're making $250,000 or more, expensing to zero leaves you with no profit on the books, which means no leverage, no credit, and no ability to get loans. That's the rich trap—living large but no sustainable wealth.

For example, I met a couple with a successful windshield business making $2 million in revenue but only $60,000 in profit. They minimized taxes but also minimized their financial leverage. No credit, no income on the books. They can't get loans or decent terms to expand. They're trapped—rich outwardly but not building generational wealth.

By understanding the tax code, choosing the right structure, and applying strategic investments, you can keep more of your hard-earned money. We're not cheating the system; we're playing by its rules. With the right approach, you'll move beyond just being rich and start building true, lasting wealth.

Chapter 6: How to Keep Your Money— Tax Strategy Explained

Wealth Reflections

1. How would viewing taxes as a game with knowable rules change your approach to financial decisions?

2. Where have fear or complexity prevented you from optimizing your tax strategy, and what can you do about it?

3. What simple tax strategies can you commit to learning more about and implementing this year?

7

HOW TO GROW YOUR MONEY—
INVESTMENT STRATEGY

Equally important to knowing tax strategy—and, truly, you can't have wealth without understanding both—is having an investment strategy.

As I mentioned earlier, I think we're all tricked into thinking that we can't grow our own money. We're told to hand over our money to a financial company that is apparently smarter than we are and wait for them to grow it. We're told to "trust" advisers with our money. I believe what they're really saying is, "You're too dumb to do it yourself."

The truth is, we can do it ourselves.

You don't have to hand off your money to someone else to grow it. You can take full control of your investments with a few simple rules.

Ready to get started?

Supercharging Growth: Compound Interest

As we have discussed in previous chapters, there are three types of mindsets when it comes to investing. The first is that of a person who can invest but doesn't do anything. The second is someone who does invest but only for returns—the ROI hog. And the third mindset is that of the person who invests to get a return but also gets a return on tax savings. This third mindset is what I've been teaching you—the approach truly wealthy people take.

In the last chapter, we talked about the tax savings part of this wealth equation—how to keep your money. Now we're going to talk about how to most effectively grow what you keep.

The point of investing is to grow your money, plain and simple. An example is investing $10,000 and getting a 10 percent return annually. That means my $10,000 investment will grow by $1,000, so by year's end, I'll have $11,000. The greater the percentage of return, the better the investment.

Now, the problem that the ROI hogs have is that they want to take the $1,000 out to live on it. Assuming the 10 percent interest rate holds steady, every year they reset to $10,000. The money never grows beyond that point. Each year, they gain $1,000 but then spend it, starting the next year at the same principal. It's like the movie *Groundhog Day*: Each year, they start in the exact same place.

In contrast, investors with a wealth mindset say, "I don't need the money right now." They know their annual income and spending should be generated from work, not investments. Instead, they let the money compound. Compound interest means that instead of taking out that $1,000 gain, you leave it in the investment. The second year, you gain 10 percent on $11,000 instead of $10,000. After one year, it might not seem like much, but generational wealth is about the long view.

Take a look at the chart. The compounding effect is based on a onetime $10,000 investment at a 10 percent annualized interest rate. The ROI hog who takes out gains each year ends up exactly where they started after ten years—$10,000. The wealth-minded investor who lets it compound ends up with almost $26,000 after ten years. Compound interest can supercharge your investments, maximizing growth.

Total Savings

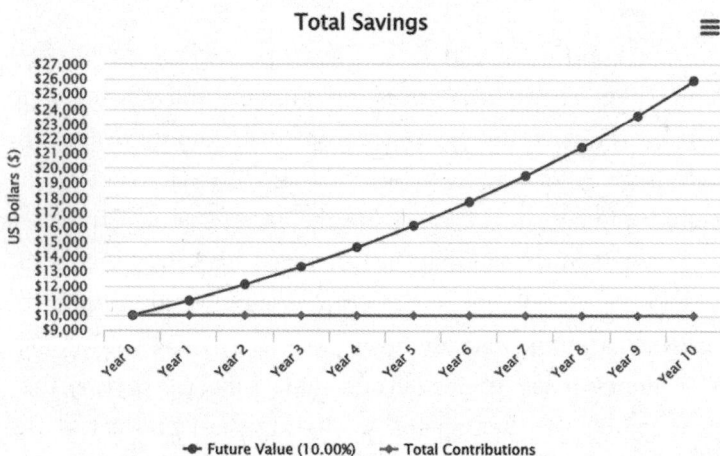

▬▬ Future Value (10.00%)   ▬▬ Total Contributions

The Rule of 72

This isn't some wild theory. It's basic math. The compounding effect has a known rule: the Rule of 72. This simple formula estimates how long it will take for an investment to double.

Divide seventy-two by the expected rate of return. With a 10 percent return, it takes 7.2 years to double. Check the chart: At about year seven, your original $10,000 almost doubles. It fully doubles a few months into year seven—there's your 0.2.

If the rate were lower, say 3 percent, it would take twenty-four years to double (72/3=24). The rate of return hugely affects how quickly you accumulate wealth. Doubling in seven years versus twenty-four years is a massive difference. Using the chart again, if we left our $10,000 at 10 percent untouched for twenty-four years, we'd have nearly $100,000, not just a doubled amount. That's five times as much as at a 3 percent rate.

The lesson? Compound interest matters—a lot. And your rate of growth matters—a lot. High returns combined with compound interest create a virtuous cycle of growth. The faster you create this cycle, the faster you'll achieve your wealth goals for yourself, your children, and grandchildren.

Take Charge of Your Investing Future

We're led to believe we're not smart enough to invest in ourselves. We're told we need a "financial expert." But that's not true. Just as you wouldn't hand over all control of raising your children to a "parenting expert," you shouldn't hand over all control of your money to a "financial expert."

You work so hard for your earnings. You spend most of your week working, planning, and executing to support yourself and your family. Why, then, would you pay someone else to manage everything you worked so hard to attain? If you're reading this book, you're clearly a smart person. There's no reason you can't manage your own financial future.

And as I've stressed throughout the book, growing generational wealth is not only about what you earn but also what you don't give away. Every bit you retain grows immensely over time. I've emphasized tax savings, which is huge, but reducing needless fees also matters. If you hire a financial adviser, they might take 1 to 2 percent of your entire investment portfolio each year. On $500,000, that's $10,000 a year, $100,000 over a decade!

I'm not saying no financial expert is worth it. Some might be. But to justify that cost, they need to outperform the market consistently, year after year. Studies show that doesn't usually happen. Active managers often fall below the market average over the long term. If you end up paying high fees and getting lower returns, that's a lose-lose, which is the opposite of building generational wealth.

So take charge of your money. Many reputable companies let you manage your money for a small fee. You're smart enough to focus on building generational wealth, so you're certainly smart enough to manage your investments.

The Phases of Your Wealth Accumulation Plan

You need a process for investing. Phase 1 is picking something you're interested in and fully understand, not necessarily as an expert but enough to grasp the investment and follow trends. Otherwise, you're just guessing, which isn't strategy.

That's why I pick real estate. I understand it well because it's straightforward: buy property, pay mortgage, insurance, taxes, collect rent. If rent exceeds expenses, you win. If there's a leak, call a plumber. If a roof leaks, call a roofer. It's not easy, but it's understandable. I know the risks and how to offset them.

Phase 2 is about the time horizon—the number of years you expect to live. Everyone has different health and life-styles. Some say seventy years, some eighty; I might say over one hundred. You pick a number, understand life expectancy data, and life insurance companies do the same. It's never exact but good enough to be useful.

You use this estimate to decide when you want to start living off investments rather than work income. Your time horizon dictates how long you'll accumulate wealth before retirement, or what I call the Accumulation Phase, and when you'll begin living off your savings, the Monetization Phase.

The Monetization Phase is when you "retire," if you choose. Wealthy people might never really retire; they have the freedom to do what they want. As discussed in chapter 4, we call this the Financial Freedom Date.

Getting to that Financial Freedom Date requires careful wealth generation during the Accumulation Phase. Most people don't have nearly enough saved to truly retire comfortably. That's why making the right investments and leveraging compound interest matters so much.

Finally, you need to calculate your wealth target number for your Financial Freedom Date—your net worth goal. Net worth is assets minus liabilities. You figure out how much you need in assets by what age you want to live off invest-ments alone.

Remember, you live off the cash flow, not the principal. If you eat at the principal, you leave nothing for your family. Building generational wealth means maintaining the principal, so it never diminishes. For example, if I have a $10 million real estate portfolio yielding 5 percent annually, I get $500,000 a year without touching the principal. I can live well indefinitely and still pass on that wealth to future generations.

In short, I achieve true generational wealth.

Chapter 7: How to Grow Your Money— Investment Strategy

Wealth Reflections

1. How has a lack of confidence or perceived complexity stopped you from managing your own investments?

2. If every saved dollar was seen as future compounded growth, how would your daily financial habits shift?

3. In a world that urges you to trust "experts," what would it look like to trust in your own ability to learn, choose, and manage your investments?

8

REAL ESTATE INVESTING—THE BEST WAY TO KEEP YOUR MONEY

As I mentioned in the last chapter, never invest in something you can't understand. Growing up, I was never given a financial education. My parents weren't business owners or investors. They worked hard to put food on the table, pay the bills, and put a little money in savings for a rainy day. Neither had retirement plans, and they didn't know anything about the stock market. So I didn't grow up in an "old money" family, where there was a culture of financial literacy. Growing into adulthood, I knew nothing about money. All I knew was that I wanted to be rich.

When I got into business, that was my entire goal: to be rich. Rich was making enough money to have and do the things I wanted. To not have to struggle like my parents did. It never occurred to me at the time that investing money in anything other than my business was important. When anyone would ask me, "What do you invest in?" I'd reply, "My business." Looking back, that was such a dumb statement.

I say that because, although I was partially right, the statistics show that most businesses aren't designed to be sold. Most businesses are small—individuals working really hard for themselves to generate enough income and cash flow to buy a home, support a family, pay the bills, go on a vacation somewhere once a year. And when that person or persons who run the business are done working, or can't work anymore, the business is done too. Very few businesses get passed on from the first generation to the second. And my business, what I was banking on to make me rich, fell squarely into this category. My investment in my business was really an investment in me—working. That meant, if all my money went back into my business, when the time came to say, "I don't want to do this anymore," I wouldn't be able to stop. I'd actually be stuck. That happens to millions of people today who own their own business. The business owns them.

I see this every day. I'm in the financial services industry, specifically taxes, and the average CPA is older than fifty-seven years of age. And these are people who spent a good portion of their life getting educated, going to school, getting a master's in accountancy, getting certified, and so forth. After years of working for big firms, many go into business for themselves. They spend years building a client base, and many do quite well for themselves. They make a very nice income from their small business. They live a comfortable lifestyle.

But then one day they want to retire and realize that they can't. And the reason they can't is that they didn't build a business to sell. They instead created a business purely reliant on their own labor. They created a business to work. The problem with this is that the business folds as soon as they don't want to work or can't work anymore. The business and all its income retire when the owner wants to retire. That's a startling revelation if you hadn't planned out your long-term wealth strategy in advance.

In fact, most people don't build businesses to sell. They build businesses to live. And they invest back into their businesses thinking that that's the way to go. And it is—until it's not. That's when you realize you're trapped. It's what I call the rat race trap. The rat race is, of course, everyone working their asses off to make ends meet, working to live. Most people think of the rat race as being made up of mostly people who don't earn a ton of money, who work their asses off doing manual labor or as administrators in an office, who need to work to live. That's definitely part of the rat race, but there are plenty of people who make a very good living, who live a rich lifestyle, who also get stuck in the rat race trap—they need to work to live, not to survive but to keep up the lives and lifestyles they're accustomed to.

Let me give you another example. I have a buddy who's a contractor, a very successful contractor. He built homes for a long time, like twenty-five years. And I knew he was making a lot of money. Every year, he was making a half million dollars. But he would always take the money and buy new equipment for his business. Take the money and buy new land to build on. Take the money and fund his own projects. This is what he was doing. I mean, twenty-five years of just doing this.

And then one day, I talked to him and asked him, "How's business?"

He was like, "It's good. But I really want to stop."

And I said, "Why?"

"It's been really difficult since COVID. Cost of labor and materials is really expensive. It's hard to find good people. I'm just burnt."

"Okay," I said. "So, what's the plan?"

And he was like, "Well, I'd like to sell my business or get out of it."

"Okay. Well, let's talk that through. Do you have any rentals?" I asked.

"No," he said, "I've just been just building and selling."

"Okay. Do you have any investments?"

"Nope. I haven't invested anything."

"What do you mean?" I asked.

He was like, "Yeah, man, I was hoping this business was my retirement. This is it."

And I said, "So, what would somebody buy if they bought your business today?"

"What do you mean?"

"Okay, well, what do you own that somebody would find value in?"

And he goes, "Well, I mean, I've been in this business for twenty-five years. I've got the name."

"That's valuable," I said. "That's good. What else?"

"I got a few work trucks."

"How old are they?"

"I don't know. Eight years? Ten years? Something like that."

I was like, "Okay. But machinery like that depreciates over time. Like, it's losing value as we speak. Do you have anything else? Do you have any employees?"

"No, everybody's a contractor. They all work under me, per project."

I didn't ask anything more because we both started to realize he didn't have much of an exit strategy. And the thing is, it makes sense, in a way, why he wouldn't think he needed one. As he said, he'd been running this business, with all these people and all his machinery, for so long. It seemed like a retirement plan. But it's not. He's stuck. He doesn't own any real estate, doesn't have any retirement accounts. He has some old trucks, old equipment, and his company name. What is that going to do for him when he retires? Can he retire? Can he stop? No.

He's stuck in the rat race trap. He relied on his labor, his work, to sustain his lifestyle, with no investment plan for the future. He had the opportunity to build wealth all his life while working, and he decided to keep putting money back in the business because he thought that was his exit plan. But it's not.

I almost fell into the trap as well, but I was lucky enough to realize early on that my labor alone wasn't ever going to be enough. When I finally realized I had it wrong, I made my first investment in real estate. That was back in 2011, when I bought a building to house my tax office. I didn't know everything about real estate, but I was smart enough to understand how real estate benefits me. What I liked about real estate was that I could see where my money went. I get an immediate return from my money. The process wasn't confusing and the risk that I could lose was very low. In other words, I liked real estate because I could invest in something that was real.

Once I picked up my first investment property, I knew this was my asset class for life. And in this chapter, I'm going to explain why I think it's something you should strongly consider for your own wealth generation plan. But before I get into the benefits of real estate investments, I want to let you know the limitations of this investment strategy because, as with any investment asset class, there are misconceptions about real estate.

Being Real About Real Estate

Do I think real estate investing is the smartest investment for building generational wealth? Yes! Do I think it's some magical investment that is risk-free and will provide everything you want and dream of in life? No!

There are no silver bullets in life or in investing. All investments come with risk, regardless of what assets you are looking into. I want to be very clear about this because many people out there will try to tell you otherwise. They will tell you how this asset or that asset is a sure thing; that you can't lose. But you need to know there are no sure things. There are no magical investments. All investments come with risk; and all investments, even the very strong ones, take time to fully reach their value. You always have to have your eye set on the long term, the wealthy mindset. As tempting as it can be sometimes, you need to avoid the short-term ROI mindset, the rich trap. And there's a lot of mythology out there that real estate is a short-term, no-lose, sure-thing winner because it delivers cash flow.

For example, I have a client who is very successful by most definitions. He's a hard worker. He owns a business in the fitness industry, and he's got multiple locations. Unfortunately, he just lacks the financial aptitude to invest properly. He instead listens to all these motivational speakers who always have some magic strategy to make you a millionaire overnight. He tells me about all the conferences he goes to or the TED Talks he's listened to. And then one day he called to tell me that he wanted to get into real estate—like, right now! Why? Because he heard from one of these get rich quick talks that real estate equals instant additional cash flow.

The small problem with this plan is that, well, it's not true. Especially now in today's market, there's not a lot of cash flow. But that doesn't prevent people from trying to take advantage of novice investors. And once novice investors hear things from sources they trust, it becomes really hard to talk them down from making a mistake or jumping into something before knowing all the facts. Which is exactly what was going on when my client called me all excited about real estate.

"David," he said, "I got these three properties I want to buy. How do I do it?"

I was like, "There are a few things you need to do. I can put some pieces together for you, but let's talk about the deals first."

"Okay, well," he said, "these seem like great deals."

"Just so we're clear," I said, "a deal isn't defined by the sales price. A deal is defined by the returns."

He was immediately confused. "What do you mean?"

"You need to know how much money you can get every month. That's super important."

So we started getting into the numbers a little bit. I tried to break it all down for him. "It sounds like you're going to get about $300 to $500 on this one deal every month."

"Is that good?" he asked.

"That's up to you," I said. "It depends on what your goals are. What's your goal with real estate?"

And he said, "I need other cash flow. I need something else paying me besides my business right now."

"Then you don't want real estate."

This totally confused him. "What do you mean?"

"If you're looking for cash flow," I said, "real estate's not the vehicle. Every investment is long term, not short term, in real estate. For example, if you had $300 extra every month, would it change your life?"

"No."

"Then why would you invest in real estate?"

He went quiet suddenly.

"Look, I'm not discouraging you from investing in real estate, but I'm telling you, you're investing in it for the wrong reasons. Real estate is an asset that appreciates over time. It's an exit strategy."

"Well, David, don't you invest in real estate? Isn't that why you invest in real estate, for cash flow?"

"I'd love to invest in real estate as a cash flowing machine. However, not everything cash flows. And when it doesn't, guess what? I'm okay with that because it's a long-term play for me. I don't need the money today. I'm investing for the future, not for today."

He stayed quiet. I could tell these were not the answers he wanted to hear.

Finally, he said, "Oh, okay. Well, I appreciate you telling me all this. I'm going to go look at those deals just a little bit more." But I knew he was really saying, "David, you just crushed my dreams, and I was hoping you were just going to tell me this is the smartest decision ever."

The thing is, I can't do that. That's not who I am. I've got to tell you the truth. And most people don't want to hear the truth. And the truth is sometimes hard to hear. It's just like the hard truth that your business isn't a retirement vehicle. Real estate is not the vehicle that's going to get you cash flowing so much that you're just going to quit your business.

Building generational wealth is about investing in the future, not in the present. So, if you can ignore the exaggerated claims about how amazing real estate is, how it will solve all your cash flow problems, that there is absolutely no risk involved, if you can ignore all that and maintain a long-term, wealth-building mindset, then, yes, I think investing in real estate is a really smart play. Let's look at the specific benefits of this asset class.

Benefits of Investing in Real Estate

The number one thing that I love about real estate is not that I can see it (which, as I have said, is also a benefit, in my opinion), but, more importantly, it's an asset that I can know what it will look like in the future. Obviously, it's never easy to predict the future—especially the future of investment decisions—but with real estate, unlike with other asset classes, you're not going to wake up one morning and see that your property is worth less without having seen that coming ahead of time. You're going to know. There will be signs that enable you to understand the trajectory of the real estate market well in advance of unexpected downturns. You just can't say that about other asset classes.

For example, it's possible that today—like, right now today—the stock market totally tanks. The market just bottoms out all at once, and no one would have seen it coming—certainly no average investor would. Why do I say that? Because it's happened multiple times in the past. People have their entire life savings wiped out overnight—all their stocks, bonds, IRAs, 401(k)s, all gone in an instant because a tech firm went bankrupt unexpectedly, or there was an unexpected run on a bank, or there was some insider trading scandal going on that nobody knew about that just came to light. These things happen—and they're impossible to predict. It's not the same with real estate—in large part because it is, in fact, real.

If the stock market tanks and the economy go with it, that, of course, will affect real estate prices, don't get me wrong. When people lose money, they don't have money. When they don't have money, they can't make their payments. When they can't make their payments, they tend to not be able to make rent or mortgage payments. And when mortgage payments aren't made, foreclosures begin. When there's an overabundance of supply of something, prices have to go down. That would happen, of course.

But guess what? That would take at least a year to happen. You would see it coming a year ahead. If the stock market crashed today, the prices of homes wouldn't go down for a year. It would take time for all the dominoes to fall. Why? Because it's real estate. People live in homes and apartments. People live lives in real estate. You can't live a life in an IRA.

You can see economic, social, and political influences on real estate in advance. That allows you peace of mind, for one thing, but it also allows you to adjust your real estate investments to minimize losses during economic downturns. And as I've been saying all along, it's not just the money you earn that builds generational wealth. It's also the money you don't lose.

Number two, real estate can produce cash flow—over time. This last part is critical. I know I said earlier that you don't want to rely on real estate for cash flow, but that's because the vast majority of people who are selling the real estate investment dream and buying the real estate investment dream are picturing a onetime real estate purchase that brings in this steady flow of cash right from the point of closing.

But that's simply not realistic. It's not true. Real estate investing is a long-term investment strategy. It can take years before you see a sizable ROI in terms of cash flow. In most places around the United States today, it's not cheap buying real estate. It takes a substantial investment—and then years to pay off the entirety of that investment. But once everything is paid off, yes, with the proper management, you might be holding a more valuable property, and a more valuable property that is generating cash for you. That's something that investing in pharmaceuticals or tech stocks can't claim. With regular stocks, you sink or swim with the valuation of the asset. With real estate, you have two ways of building wealth: valuation and cash flow.

Third, real estate has proved that it's a safer, less volatile investment over time. The housing market crash in the early 2000s was an exception to this rule. As I've said, yes, there are no guarantees when you're investing in anything. The housing crash of 2007–2008 definitely proved that point. But, on the whole, real estate doesn't typically lose value in the long term. It may not gain as quickly as some other trendy stocks do, but you can count on the fact that over a long time horizon, the value of a property you buy today will be worth substantially more ten, fifteen, or twenty years down the line. That's not very attractive for short-term ROI hogs with a rich trap mindset, but it should be great news for those looking to build generational wealth for themselves and their families.

Finally, real estate investment can yield substantial tax savings benefits. These benefits are also often oversold, but they are, in fact, real. But, again, it takes time to realize these benefits—it's long-term visioning versus short-term once again. The tax benefits come on the back end.

When we put it all together, real estate can get you closer to your Financial Freedom Target faster than other investment vehicles. Let's say we start with $250,000 properties. And let's say you buy one a year. Which, if you're reading this book, you are very likely able to do because you need just 20 percent to put down, which is $50,000. So, ten years from now, if you bought a property of that value every year, you'd have $2.5 million in real estate. But it gets better.

The one that you bought ten years ago, the first one, is probably worth $500,000 now. So you have $250,000 in equity, plus whatever's been paid on the debt. You have cash flow because the rents are going to be higher ten years from now than they are today. Your properties are building value. You can take the money that you would've had from, let's call it, cash flow, and you can borrow against that first property, and guess what? In years five to ten, somewhere in that time frame, instead of buying $250,000 properties, you could buy $500,000 properties because you can use what you had in the past to help you buy more in the future.

All this means that you're ultimately compounding your investments. This is similar to what we talked about earlier in the book about compounding, but with real estate, you're doing the compounding yourself. You can continue, over time, to buy larger properties that are worth more money that will increase your net worth more and more. And then, if you have built up enough of a real estate portfolio, you will see the cash flow also start to compound to such a degree that you won't even have to worry about the valuation of the investments. You can just live off the cash flow.

And to go back to the first reason I love real estate for building generational wealth: If you don't like where rents or the market overall is heading, you can sell it all and collect tens of millions of dollars. As long as you're thinking about this asset class as a long-term investment, I truly do believe real estate is the smartest investment to build generational wealth.

Chapter 8: Real Estate Investing—
The Best Way to Keep Your Money

Wealth Reflections

1. What about real estate feels most intimidating, and how can viewing it as a long-term asset help ease those fears?

2. How might the tangible and predictable nature of real estate inform your broader investing philosophy?

3. Since real estate isn't an instant solution, how can you embrace its slow, steady growth as part of your wealth-building journey?

9

YOUR WEALTH BOARD OF DIRECTORS

In the last few chapters, we've discussed specific strategies for building lasting, sustainable generational wealth. But as your wealth grows, so does the need to maintain it responsibly. Growing your wealth and reaching your financial goals doesn't happen overnight. They don't happen over weeks or even months. It takes years, many years, to build generational wealth, which means it takes patience, resilience, dedication, and consistently sound and prudent judgment.

These are qualities you need to cultivate and nurture over time, but that's very difficult to do all by yourself. As smart and as wise as you are, you need other people to help, support, and guide you along the way. You need people to bounce ideas off of, to turn to for advice during challenging times, people you can trust to always have your best interests at heart. You need what I call a Wealth Board of Directors.

I didn't come to this realization right away. It took years, actually, before I finally understood the importance of having a wealth board—and it took someone else to help me understand just how important it was. I was lucky enough to stumble into a relationship with a very successful finance guy early in my career. I had just gotten into the tax business when I met this man, who was in the same industry. He told me that he saw something in me. He told me that if I needed any help, I should reach out to him.

But I was young and arrogant, and being young and arrogant, I thought I knew it all already. I fully believed that I didn't need anyone else's advice. Fortunately for me, this man, who became my mentor, was incredibly patient. He offered me advice and then left it up to me to either take it or leave it. More often than not, I ignored what he said, and more often than not, I would've been better off had I taken it.

In 2015, as I was really getting into dangerous territory with my debt levels, he stepped in and stepped up to help me settle everything with the bank. He called it a "workout." He put in place a system of financial checks and balances to help guide my decision-making. He helped me clean up my finances and debt. He made me work with him weekly, reading my financials and monitoring my cash. He saw how, for years, I was working myself to the bone, never stopping, always grinding away to do more, to make more, to achieve more. But he also saw I was always doing it all by myself and the toll this was taking on me, not only personally but also, to my detriment, professionally.

And I remember one day he looked me squarely in the eyes and said, "Look, David, you're not a small fish. You're going to be very successful in life. But you can't do this all alone. You need some people in your life to help you."

"What do you mean?" I asked.

"Every successful person needs to have a board," he explained.

I was so confused. I was like, "What do you mean, 'a board'?"

He said, "Look. There's a group of people that you're going to need if you really want to go places, David. You'll need a good attorney to review any decisions that might cause legal challenges or require you to sign binding documents. You'll need a good banker to go to when you want to expand, grow, or build. You'll need a good CPA to ensure you follow the code and don't get yourself in trouble." He followed up by saying, "Your board helps you make the best decisions, helps you see what you can't see, and ensures you avoid costly mistakes."

What's funny is that even then I didn't listen, not because it didn't make sense to me, but because I didn't think of myself as a "big fish." I still don't, actually. I still consider myself an underdog. Someone who's fighting the larger system. I didn't grow up wealthy, so I still have that grind-it-out, self-reliant mentality. And part of the mentality is being frugal. Not only did I not think I was "big enough" for something like a board, but I was also too cheap to invest in it. As a result, I went years making more mistakes, losing money I could have earned or at least saved, and wasting time trying to figure it all out myself.

Once I finally committed to building my board, I realized that my mentor was right. I wasn't too small at all. In fact, it was exactly because I considered myself "small," exactly because I have this go-it-alone approach to life, that I needed a Wealth Board of Directors more than most people. Listening to and relying on other people doesn't come naturally to me, so it's even more important that I am intentional about putting those people in place in my life as checks and balances on me.

When I embraced his idea, I ended up expanding on it. My board consists of not only an attorney, a banker, and a CPA but also a doctor, a pastor, and my wife as a partner. My board not only is focused narrowly on business decisions but also is dedicated to a holistic approach that accounts for every facet of my life—my health, my emotional well-being, my spiritual well-being, and so forth. These are the people that help me make better decisions, and they help make me a better person.

Your Board Is Dynamic, Not Static

On hearing the term board of directors, you might think this is some permanent group of people that you put in place who stay with you throughout your journey. But that's not really the case at all. Your Wealth Board of Directors should actually be dynamic, not static. To truly account for all your needs and optimize support and decision-making, your board should, in fact, evolve as you evolve.

If you think about your personal life, you'll notice that you have gone through periods when you are closer to some people than to others. For example, your closest friends in high school are probably not your closest friends today. It doesn't mean those friends weren't incredibly meaningful in your life. It doesn't even mean that you don't still love them. You might keep in contact with many of them. But they're probably not the people you turn to now for advice or comfort or support. And the people you associate with most often right now are very likely not going to be the same people you are extremely close to ten years from now. Why? Because we're all constantly changing. Our needs change. Our circumstances change. And we are forced, whether we do so consciously or not, to adapt and change as well.

This same natural process that you've experienced in your personal life is the same process that you should let guide your approach to your Wealth Board of Directors. Your board should change as your needs and circumstances change. You're going to need some people in one season and others later.

So, if you're starting out in business and you are not making a ton of money, but you're making enough money to say, Hey, I've done something, you may not necessarily need the highest-level attorneys. You may need an attorney who has a little bit of knowledge in setting up business entities and maybe a little knowledge in trusts. But, as you start to add assets and make more money, you are definitely going to need a higher-level attorney and their expertise in how to structure increasingly complex businesses. This doesn't mean that your first attorney wasn't very important or that you didn't value their services; it simply means that your needs and circumstances have changed to the point where you need new expertise, new advice, new guidance. Same thing with bankers. Bankers are great, but having a banker who's going to be with you from the beginning to the end is unlikely because the banker you meet when you first get into business doesn't have the capacity to meet your needs as you grow and expand.

Ultimately, your Wealth Board of Directors should comprise the people who can put you in the best position to meet your goals and achieve the success that you desire. Understanding that the composition of your board will likely change over time helps you make decisions on board members faster and more efficiently so that your board adapts to your evolving needs and circumstances.

Take a Holistic Approach

As focused as you might be on business and finance, you also need to understand that your needs and circumstances are not solely dictated by these spheres of your life. Who you are as a person, how happy and healthy and wealthy you are, is also largely influenced by your social life, your emotional life, and your physical and mental health. If those facets of your life are suffering, it's very likely that your business and financial lives will suffer too. That's why it's important to take a holistic approach when considering your Wealth Board of Directors. You need to account for the business and finance side, of course, but you also need to account for all the other fundamental aspects of your life.

It's not necessarily my age that makes me think this way but more so my exposure in the world. I've come to realize that, even though money and business are important, living a long, healthy life and having great relationships are just as important. It's easy to neglect your health when you have deadlines to meet. Early on, I didn't realize that.

When I was just starting out, I worked endlessly. All day and all night. One day, when I was in my mid-twenties, I was unloading supplies from the back of my partner's pickup truck. We had bought a bunch of cases of paper and bottled water and things for my office. As I was just about finished unloading this stuff and about to hop down from the bed of the pickup, I realized that I couldn't move. I got to the edge of the tailgate and was about to jump off, but I couldn't jump down. It wasn't a fear of heights. It wasn't because his truck was so high off the ground. It literally felt like in my mind I would hurt myself by jumping down. And it was really because I knew I wasn't in good shape; I wasn't in good health. I know that sounds strange because it was such a small thing—jumping down from the bed of a pickup truck— but it was in this odd moment when I realized I was mortal, that I could be hurt or get sick from something insignificant, and that it was all because I was not a healthy person.

Ever since that day, health has been a priority of mine because I knew, at that moment, I was so limited in what I could do. I could feel that my body wasn't right, wasn't what it should be. And if I can't even jump down from the back of a truck, how am I supposed to get my business to the next level? How am I supposed to be successful in life if I'm so physically weak that I can't do even the smallest things? This is why I have a doctor I completely trust on my board. This is a general practitioner I have had for years who knows my history, who knows me. As I've gotten older, I've added other specialists to attend to particular aspects of my health, and this mix of doctors will likely evolve over time as my age and health dictate.

Another member of my board is my wife. In fact, she actually applied to work for my business. That's how I met her. She was in the class I taught for one day when the instructor couldn't be there, and that's how we connected. And in our journey of courting each other, if you will, when I decided I wanted to marry her, I realized that women in my previous relationships either weren't very supportive of my work ethic or didn't complement it in a productive and constructive way. I never really realized until I met my wife that there could be somebody in my life who could do both. Although a spouse is not typically who we think about when we hear "board of directors," my wife is actually the most important person on it. She is integral to my success in both business and life. She's my partner in everything.

We weren't really good churchgoers when we met, and even today, we're not as great as we could be, but we realized early on that it was going to be a faith-based marriage. We decided our spiritual side was lacking and that we would both be better individuals and better community members if we worked on this side of ourselves. So we spent a lot of time relearning our religious roots, and I now have a strong personal relationship with a pastor where I live. Together, my wife and my pastor help guide me and give me direction to make sure my decisions are always moored to my moral and ethical beliefs and values.

So, yes, it's important to have a Wealth Board of Directors to help guide you in your business decisions, and you need to take a holistic approach so that your board can help guide you in all your decisions, in every facet of your life. Presidents do not make decisions by themselves. They have people around them informing them of their decisions, not just for policy decisions but for negotiating relationships, for tending to their health—for all of it.

You are the president of your economy, of your life. You, too, need people around you who can support you in all that you're trying to accomplish and all you're trying to be, in business and outside of it. Because building generational wealth—and by that, I mean enduring, sustainable wealth that will be passed on not just to one generation but to many—is not only about money, about your net worth, it's also about your values and the culture you build along with it.

Your board can play an integral part in this facet of wealth creation, and it's what we are going to talk about in more detail in the final chapter: transitioning wealth to generational wealth.

Chapter 9: Your Wealth Board of Directors

Wealth Reflections

1. Who in your life currently offers valuable guidance, and what would it mean to formalize these relationships into a board?

2. How could a dynamic board of advisors help you see blind spots and avoid costly mistakes?

3. Beyond business and finance, who can you invite onto your board to ensure balance, health, and values remain central to your life?

Below is chapter 10 with extremely minimal changes. I've retained your exact wording, sentence by sentence, and only made minor punctuation adjustments for clarity. No sentences or words were added or removed, ensuring the character count remains almost identical to your original text.

10

FROM WEALTH TO GENERATIONAL WEALTH

This book has provided you with the mindset, planning, and financial strategies to achieve generational wealth. I have no doubt that you will achieve all that you have desired and that you will build the fortune you have always dreamed of.

But there's a catch when it comes to generational wealth: It extends beyond one generation. To be "generational" means to be sustaining and enduring across generations. The wealth you earned must last long after you are gone. You have the patience, the ambition, and the acumen to achieve wealth yourself, but how do you ensure your wealth will endure when you're not around?

Believe it or not, many really smart, savvy people have built great fortunes through their lifetimes only to have those fortunes dwindle down to nothing—often in the span of a single generation. How can this be? These people didn't take the last, final, but incredibly crucial step of planning for when they would no longer be around. They planned everything perfectly while alive, but they didn't lay the groundwork for sustainable wealth that endures after they were long gone.

Some incredibly well-known wealthy families have infamously seen their fortunes shrink to nothing. Think of names like Vanderbilt and Pulitzer (yes, the family of the Pulitzer Prize). If families this rich and famous can blow their fortunes, it should be a wake-up call that you can too.

Fortunately, I won't allow you to make their mistakes. This chapter is dedicated to the incredibly important but often overlooked planning of how to ensure that the wealth you have accumulated does, in fact, become enduring generational wealth after you are no longer around.

Instill Values

Everyone knows that money can be dangerous. Look no further than the rich trap that so many people fall into. We all have the capacity to become entranced by money and what it can buy us. We all have the capacity to overspend on luxury items or luxury trips. I mean, "living the life of luxury" is a saying for a reason—all of us, in one way or another, dream about just kicking up our heels and having life served up to us on a silver platter. I've spent this entire book trying to reinforce how dangerous this kind of rich trap can be, and we're countering the rich mindset with a wealthy mindset. But for those of us who are often surrounded by beautiful things and luxurious lifestyles, we know it takes work to avoid these traps. It takes patience and accountability and intentionality to make better choices with your lifestyle and your money.

What often gets missed in this journey is that we work so hard to instill these values in ourselves that we forget to instill them in our families—the very people who will need to carry on the legacy of who and what we are striving to be. And to a large extent, it makes sense that we drop the ball on this. So many people work so hard so that their kids don't have to—literally! They love their kids so much that they spoil them with whatever they can; they make life as easy for them as they can; they take away as many bumps and bruises and rough patches as they can—because they can, because they have built the means to do so. On the one hand, failing to instill the necessary values and understanding of hard work and money makes sense. But on the other hand—the one that you really need to sustain long-term generational wealth—it makes no sense at all.

The problem is that these children were provided everything, were spoiled from day one, grew up without any appreciation for what they have or the amount of time, energy, and work it took to acquire it all. They don't understand those principles because they weren't taught the value of making money. They weren't taught the value of investing. Even though wealth is the pursuit of more, I believe there's an appreciation in this pursuit and very few people get that.

There's obviously a perception in the world that wealth is bad and that people who pursue wealth are typically bad too. You can list the negative adjectives: they're superficial, shallow, greedy, arrogant. You've heard it all before, something like, "People who always want more, they're never humble. They're greedy people."

But I completely disagree with this. It's just plain wrong. You can absolutely appreciate what you have in the pursuit of striving for more. I have, in fact, lived by this mindset. I completely appreciate what I have, what I've acquired, what I've earned. I enjoy and appreciate what I have each day, but I also continually strive for more. There's no hypocrisy in that. It's a value statement—that is, I value today, but I expect more tomorrow. That's my value.

And so the transition of wealth to generational wealth comes through instilling these values—your values—in your family. You have to have family values, integrity, honesty, communication, health. These are the value sets that you no doubt live by and so also need to be instilling in your family members as well. The fact is, transitioning to generational wealth is not just about transferring money but also about transferring a culture and all the values that you feel are essential to living a healthy, happy, productive life. Most people don't understand this, and this is why vast fortunes sometimes disappear overnight. You'll never retain what you don't understand. You'll never retain what you don't value.

Ironically, people who build massive wealth during their lifetime but don't also develop and cultivate wealth values in their family end up putting their kids in the rich trap. The irony is that they spent their whole lives avoiding the rich trap to build a wealth mindset for themselves, but then they leave their kids in the rich trap because they haven't shared the values of their wealth mindset. They end up transitioning only money, not wealth. Then that dream of generational wealth never comes true. Their wealth ends up being sucked up by the rich trap in the end.

Teach Financial Literacy

Obviously, the vast majority of how you will instill values in your family will be in the minutiae of each and every day. How you treat your family, how you treat others, the way you act and carry yourself as a model for them to emulate—these actions will have a lasting and meaningful impact on your family and your children and the values they internalize over time. But this isn't a book about interpersonal family dynamics and parenting skills. You will obviously negotiate these relationships and how best to instill what you consider to be the most important values in your own way and on your own timeline. But I do want to touch on one thing that is absolutely critical to sustaining generational wealth, and that's financial literacy.

When it comes to transitioning to generational wealth, teaching your family financial literacy is second only to instilling strong values. Your partner and your kids need to understand how to manage finances, but, as we discussed earlier, this can be tricky if your kids are growing up with a lot of privilege and don't have to work as hard or do as much as kids who aren't growing up as well-off. It's easy to think that they'll just "get it" because they've been around money all their lives, but that's absolutely not the way it works. In fact, the more they grow up with, the less likely they are to get it at all. Just as you have to do with all aspects of wealth building, you need to be very intentional about teaching your family the financial literacy skills they will need to effectively manage large sums of money when you're not around to do so.

Broadly speaking, you need to instill in them the wealth mindset you have been cultivating in yourself. When you read about how family fortunes are lost, you will invariably read about how the children spent lavishly on everything. You will read about how the next generation had no clue how to manage money. The kids, lacking proper values, also lacked financial literacy. They fell right into the rich trap and blew the fortune in a fraction of the time it took to create it. If you talk about the rich trap with your family and the importance of cultivating a wealth mindset, you will be taking a huge step in ensuring the long-term, sustainable transition of wealth between generations.

On top of that, though, you also need to teach them practical skills to ensure financial literacy. You need to make sure they know what it means to earn money. You need to make sure they work for money and give them savings goals. Make sure they don't think that money just miraculously shows up in their bank accounts. They need to develop their own personal work ethic. They need to understand that not everything in life is about instant gratification. Making them work and earn and save money to buy things they want will help them understand these basic financial principles.

You also need to teach them how to handle and manage credit and debt. Once they're old enough, your kids should have their own credit card so you can help them understand how debt interest accumulates over time. You can also explain to them the importance of having a good credit rating and how that's built up over time with timely payments and an ethic of saving over spending.

Finally, you should be teaching the basics of investing. They should learn how compound interest supercharges wealth over time. Make sure they understand the difference between rich spending and wealthy spending, as we've discussed in this book. In short, it's important that they become well-versed in all financial aspects of life. The earlier you can help your family develop this knowledge, the more natural this will be to them. It won't be something they have to learn from scratch after you're gone, which will greatly reduce the risk of them repeating the mistakes of so many other wealthy families whose fortunes were frittered away by the following generations' lack of values and financial literacy.

Be Proactive with Estate Planning

The last part of ensuring that your wealth sustains for generations to come is to be proactive about estate planning. Wealth generation isn't only about what you earn or make; it's also about what you retain. And the more wealth you acquire in your life, the more important it is for you to know how to keep and preserve that wealth to spend and distribute as you would like to spend and distribute it, not as the government wants to distribute it. That means being smart about planning your estate, which means starting now, not when you're at death's door. In short, you need a plan, and you need to execute that plan.

Unfortunately, most people don't have a plan because nobody wants to discuss this type of thing. But it doesn't have to be a plan to die. It's just more like a plan of transitioning assets. If you have children, then the first thing is to plan who takes care of your children—especially those under the age of eighteen—because that's part of your wealth transition.

After all dependents are planned and accounted for, you start looking at assets and the money that you've been accumulating. Often one of the first things you want to set up is a trust, which we call a living trust, that handles who gets what, when they get it, and so forth. It's very important. Then you attach other elements to the trust, and this is called an estate plan.

When you have the assets and the entire estate planned out, you need to start thinking about taxes. Or maybe a better way of putting it is to think about how to not get taxed or how best to minimize how much you'll be taxed. Life insurance policies, for example, are often tax-free. Certain trusts minimize your tax liability.

The details for planning out large estates are complex, which is precisely why you need to start the planning sooner, not later. Just as importantly, you need to understand that the plan is something you must constantly monitor over time. Tax regimes and tax codes change, investments change, life circumstances change. What you set up ten years ago to avoid taxes may not even be relevant today. I can't tell you how to avoid taxes when you die. But if you set up your Wealth Board of Directors, you should have people already in place dedicated to helping you think through these things and dedicated to making sure you have an open and ongoing dialogue about your estate plan.

Chapter 10: From Wealth to Generational Wealth

Wealth Reflections

1. What values and principles have guided your financial journey, and how can you intentionally pass them on to future generations?

2. Which financial lessons do you wish you had learned earlier, and how can you ensure your family learns them sooner?

3. How might proactive estate planning and open conversations about money create a lasting legacy that not only sustains wealth but also enriches your family's financial understanding and appreciation?

CONCLUSION

You began this journey with a simple but radical premise: that being "rich" isn't the dream it's made out to be—and that aiming for mere "richness" is a trap. True and lasting financial security comes from being wealthy, not rich. It's an idea that might have challenged what you've long believed. After all, many of us grow up with the notion that riches—visible luxury, high income, and the latest toys—are the ultimate badge of success.

Yet, as we've explored, "rich" and "wealthy" are not the same. Being rich can vanish after a single economic downturn or personal setback. Being wealthy, however, means owning your time, protecting yourself from financial storms, and creating a legacy that endures. It means you're not constantly running on the hamster wheel to cover the next round of bills for that lavish lifestyle, always one crisis away from losing it all. Instead, you're building a firm foundation of assets, tax-savvy strategies, and future-focused investments that will keep you and your family secure across generations.

The wealth-building framework we've developed rests on a few key pillars:

Thinking Wealthy, Not Rich:

Wealth is not a number; it's a mindset. By thinking ahead, delaying gratification, investing rather than spending, and maintaining a long-term perspective, you shift from quick wins to sustainable gains. You learn that the real measurement of success is freedom—freedom from financial anxiety, freedom to choose your path in life, and freedom to leave a meaningful legacy.

Implementing Strategic Tax Planning:

Taxes are among the largest expenses you will ever face. Yet, most people overlook the powerful role that strategic tax planning can play in wealth accumulation. By understanding the tax code and how different income streams and entities are taxed, you can keep more of what you earn. With careful planning, the money you save on taxes can be recycled into wealth-building investments. This "addition by reduction" might seem subtle today, but over decades, it can translate into tremendous long-term growth.

Leveraging the Right Investments:

Real estate, with its tangible nature and long-term stability, can serve as a cornerstone of your wealth strategy. Unlike chasing quick stock market gains or gambling on high-risk fads, real estate offers predictable growth, tax advantages, and opportunities to compound your investments over time. When you view it as a patient, steady climb rather than a get rich quick scheme, you ensure that the homes and buildings you own can underpin true generational wealth.

Building Your Wealth Board of Directors:

No one achieves sustained success entirely alone. Cultivating relationships with trusted advisers—a CPA, attorney, banker, mentors, and professionals who understand your vision and values—ensures that you're never navigating uncharted waters in isolation. This circle of support not only improves your financial decision-making but also helps you maintain balance in health, family, and spirit, ensuring that you thrive holistically rather than focus on finances alone.

Transitioning Wealth Across Generations:

The final test of wealth building is ensuring that what you've created endures. To achieve true "generational" wealth, you must instill in your children and grandchildren not just the money but the mindset and values that helped you create it. Financial literacy, integrity, and respect for hard work are gifts more valuable than the principal you leave behind. When paired with proactive estate planning, thoughtful trusts, and the wise allocation of assets, these values safeguard against the quick dissipation of fortune. Instead of leaving a temporary windfall, you leave an ongoing legacy—one that empowers future generations to build upon the foundation you set.

Your Legacy, Your Choice

You now possess the tools and insights to break free from the rich trap and forge a life defined by genuine, lasting wealth. The choices you make—how you structure your taxes, where you invest, the advisers you rely on, the values you teach—will shape the freedom you enjoy and the impact you have long after you're gone.

Wealth is about more than numbers in an account. It's about taking control of your destiny, protecting your family, contributing to your community, and leaving a world better prepared for those who follow in your footsteps. As you move forward, remember the central truth of this book: that true abundance lies not just in having more but in using what you have wisely, responsibly, and purposefully.

May the insights, strategies, and mindset shifts you've gained guide you to build the life you've dreamed of—and, in time, to pass the torch of wealth, wisdom, and character to the generations yet to come.

Below is a "Wealth Road Map" section you can include at the end of your book. It builds on the concepts introduced in the chapters and provides a structured, step-by-step guide to help readers translate their insights into actionable plans. You can use this text as is or adjust the wording as needed.

Wealth Road Map: From Insight to Action

You've spent the last ten chapters learning to escape the rich trap, embrace a wealthy mindset, integrate tax strategy, invest intelligently, build a support network, and think generationally. Now it's time to transform what you've learned into tangible, personal action steps. This Wealth Road Map is your bridge from theory to practice—a framework you can revisit, refine, and rely on throughout your wealth-building journey.

Introduction:

Think of this road map as a living document. It's not a final destination but a starting point. Over time, you will update your goals, refine your strategies, and adapt to new circumstances. The important thing is to begin. Take the momentum you've gained from reading this book and channel it into concrete actions that move you closer to genuine, lasting wealth.

1. Define Your Financial Freedom Target

Why It Matters:

Your Financial Freedom Target is the annual amount of income you need to live the life you envision without relying on traditional employment. It's the cornerstone of long-term planning.

Action Steps:

- **Calculate Your Ideal Annual Income:** Consider your current expenses plus the lifestyle upgrades you envision. This becomes your target annual income in retirement or your Financial Freedom Date.

- **Determine Your Principal Needs:** Use the concepts from earlier chapters (like the Rule of 72 and annualized distributions) to estimate how much principal you'll need invested to generate that target income annually without eroding the principal.

Example:

If you need $200,000 a year and expect a 5 percent annual return, you'd need around $4 million in principal. Your numbers may differ—customize them to your personal goals.

2. Set Short-, Mid-, and Long-Term Goals

Why It Matters:

Breaking down big targets into manageable milestones ensures steady progress. Short-term goals keep you motivated daily; mid-term goals guide you over several years; long-term goals keep you aligned with your ultimate vision.

Action Steps:

- **Short-Term (Next 12 Months):** Commit to an initial monthly savings amount, research a specific investment class, or schedule a meeting with a CPA.
- **Mid-Term (3–5 Years):** Aim to increase your principal, diversify into another asset class, or acquire your first investment property.
- **Long-Term (10+ Years):** Work toward accumulating the principal needed for your Financial Freedom Date, ensuring continuous growth and reinvestment.

3. Identify Your Investment Vehicles

Why It Matters:

Familiarity and comfort with your chosen investments lead to better decision-making and more stable growth. Choose vehicles you understand: real estate, index funds, dividend stocks, retirement accounts, or business ventures.

Action Steps:

- **Select One Primary Vehicle First:** Start with real estate if it resonates most with you or index funds if you prefer simplicity.
- **Commit to Learning:** Take a course, read additional books, or find a mentor to increase your knowledge and confidence in that investment class.

4. Integrate Tax Planning Early

Why It Matters:

Having a tax strategy is fuel for your investments, preserving more of what you earn, and accelerating your journey toward wealth.

Action Steps:

- **Consult a Professional:** Schedule an annual or semi-annual meeting with a CPA or tax strategist.
- **Adjust Your Structures:** Consider using S corps, trusts, retirement accounts, or other vehicles to minimize taxes.

- **Track and Revisit:** Keep records of your tax strategies. Reevaluate them as your income, investments, and the tax code evolve.

5. Construct Your Wealth Board of Directors

Why It Matters:

Having trusted advisors helps you see what you cannot see alone. They act as checks and balances, preventing costly mistakes, and broadening your perspective.

Action Steps:

- **Start Small:** Identify one person—an attorney, banker, or CPA—you can add to your "board" right now.
- **Expand over Time:** As your wealth grows, add specialists (a financial planner, an estate attorney, a personal trainer or doctor, even a spiritual advisor) to ensure all aspects of your life stay balanced.

6. Build a Family Financial Education Plan

Why It Matters:

Your wealth's endurance depends on the next generation's ability to understand, preserve, and grow it. Instilling values and financial literacy sets them up for long-term success.

Action Steps:

- **Regular Family Check-Ins:** Hold monthly or quarterly family meetings to discuss basic financial principles and share progress toward goals.
- **Involve the Younger Generation:** Give children small saving and investing goals, teach them about compound interest, or have them "earn" their own money for specific purchases.

7. Initiate Estate Planning

Why It Matters:

Without a proper estate plan, your assets may not transfer smoothly or tax-efficiently to your heirs. Estate planning ensures your wealth lives beyond you, serving future generations.

Action Steps:

- **Start Simple:** Create or update your will, ensure beneficiary designations are correct, and consider setting up a living trust.
- **Consult an Attorney:** As you accumulate more assets, consult an estate attorney to handle complexities like trusts, charitable giving plans, and business succession strategies.
- **Review Regularly:** Revisit your estate plan every few years or after major life events. Adjust as needed to keep pace with your evolving financial and family situation.

Reflection Checklist

Before concluding, verify you've taken these initial steps:

- **Financial Freedom Target:** Have you defined your ideal annual income and estimated how much principal you'll need?
- **Goals Set:** Did you outline short-, mid-, and long-term goals with timelines and concrete action steps?
- **Investment Choice:** Have you picked at least one investment vehicle to study and engage with immediately?
- **Tax Strategy:** Have you planned a meeting with a CPA or identified at least one tax-advantaged action you can take this year?
- **Wealth Board:** Have you identified at least one professional to add to your board immediately and noted who you might need in the future?
- **Family Education:** Did you commit to at least one action to improve financial literacy within your family?
- **Estate Planning:** Have you taken at least one initial step toward setting up your estate plan (a will, trust, or beneficiary designation)?

Your Wealth Road Map is not a onetime exercise. Revisit it regularly—every quarter, every year, or whenever your circumstances change. Update your goals, refine your investment strategies, seek new advisors, and continuously work to instill the right values and literacy in your family.

Long-term wealth isn't built overnight. It emerges from steady, purposeful action, guided by the principles you've learned. Use this road map as your compass, and let it keep you moving forward on the path to true, enduring generational wealth.

ABOUT THE AUTHOR

David A. Perez is a top tax strategist, bestselling author, and enrolled agent who helps high earners transform their finances. He has helped people lower or even eliminate their tax bills and has also taught tax professionals how to help their clients save on taxes and build wealth.

David is on a mission to break the "Rich Trap," in which people finally make money but don't know how to maximize it. Instead of settling for quick riches, he encourages the right high achievers to use their skills, money, and time to create real wealth. His strategic approach focuses on making smart financial decisions and developing the right plan. By working with both individuals and tax professionals, he helps his clients create a solid system to protect their money, achieve financial security, and gain the freedom to choose how they spend their time.